the lilaguide

by PARENTS *for* PARENTS

baby-friendly cleveland

NEW PARENT SURVIVAL GUIDE TO SHOPPING, ACTIVITIES, RESTAURANTS AND MORE...

1ST EDITION

LOCAL EDITOR: RENEE MORGAN

PUBLISHED BY THE LILAGUIDE/OAM SOLUTIONS, INC.
SAN FRANCISCO, CA   WWW.LILAGUIDE.COM

Published by:
OAM Solutions, Inc.
139 Saturn Street
San Francisco, CA 94114, USA
415.252.1300
orders@lilaguide.com
www.lilaguide.com

ISBN. 1-932847-15-4
First Printing: 2005
Printed in the USA
Copyright © 2005 by OAM Solutions, Inc.

table of contents

No, for the last time, the baby does not come with a handbook. And even if there were a handbook, you wouldn't read it. You'd fill out the warranty card, throw out the box, and start playing right away. Until a few hours passed and you were hit with the epiphany of, "Gee whiz honey, what in the wide, wide world of childcare are we doing here?"

Relax. We had that panicked thought when we had our daughter Delilah. And so did **all the parents** we talked to when they had their children. And while we all knew there was no handbook, there was, we found, a whole lot of **word-of-mouth information**. Everyone we talked to had some bit of child rearing advice about what baby gear store is the most helpful. Some **nugget of parenting wisdom** about which restaurant tolerates strained carrots on the floor. It all really seemed to help. Someone, we thought, should write this down.

And that's when, please pardon the pun, the lilaguide was born. The book you're now holding is a guide **written by local parents for local parents**. It's what happens when someone actually does write it down (and organizes it, calculates it, and presents it in an easy-to-use format).

Nearly 1,700 surveys have produced this first edition of **the lilaguide: Baby-Friendly Cleveland**. It provides a truly unique insider's view of over 650 "parent-friendly" stores, activities, restaurants, and service providers that are about to become a very big part of your life. And while this guide won't tell you how to change a diaper or how to get by on little or no sleep (that's what grandparents are for), it will tell you what other **local parents have learned** about the amazing things your city and neighborhood have to offer.

As you peruse these reviews, please remember that this guide is **not intended to be a comprehensive directory** since it does not contain every baby store or activity in the area. Rather, it is intended to provide a short-list of places that your neighbors and friends **deemed exciting and noteworthy**. If a place or business is not listed, it simply means that nobody (or not enough people) rated or submitted information about it to us. **Please let us know** about your favorite parent and baby-friendly businesses and service providers by participating in our online survey at **www.lilaguide.com**. We always want your opinions!

So there you have it. Now go make some phone calls, clean up the house, take a nap, or do something on your list before the baby arrives.

Enjoy!

Oli & Elysa

Oli Mittermaier & Elysa Marco, MD

PS

We love getting feedback (good and bad) so don't be bashful. Email us at **lila@lilaguide.com** with your thoughts, comments and suggestions. We'll be sure to try to include them in next year's edition!

We'd like to take a moment to offer a heart-felt thank you to all the **parents who participated in our survey** and took the time to share their thoughts and opinions. Without your participation, we would never have been able to create this unique guide.

Thanks also to **Lisa Barnes**, **Nora Borowsky**, **Todd Cooper**, **Amy Iannone**, **Katy Jacobson**, **Felicity John Odell**, **Shira Johnson**, **Kasia Kappes**, **Jen Krug**, **Dana Kulvin**, **Deborah Schneider**, **Kevin Schwall**, **April Stewart**, and **Nina Thompson** for their tireless editorial eyes, **Satoko Furuta** and **Paul D. Smith** for their beautiful sense of design, and **Lane Foard** for making the words yell.

Special thanks to **Paul D. Smith**, **Ken Miles**, and **Ali Wing** for their consistent support and overall encouragement in all things lilaguide, and of course **our parents** for their unconditional support in this and all our other endeavors.

And last, but certainly not least, thanks to **little Delilah** for inspiring us to embark on this challenging, yet incredibly fulfilling project.

thank yous

disclaimer

This book is designed to share parents' opinions regarding baby-related products, services and activities. It is sold with the understanding that the information contained in the book **does not represent the publisher's opinion** or recommendations.

The reviews contained in this guide are based on **public opinion surveys** and are therefore subjective in nature. The publisher shall have neither liability nor responsibility to any person or entity with respect to any loss or damage caused, or alleged to have been caused, directly or indirectly, by the information contained in this book.

ratings

Most listings have stars and numbers as part of their write-up. These symbols mean the following:

❺ / ★★★★★	extraordinary
❹ / ★★★★☆	very good
❸ / ★★★☆☆	good
❷ / ★★☆☆☆	fair
❶ / ★☆☆☆☆	poor
✓	available
✗	not available/relevant

If a ⭐ is listed instead of ★, it means that the rating is less reliable because a small number of parents surveyed the listing. Furthermore, if a listing has **no stars** or **criteria ratings**, it means that although the listing was rated, the number of surveys submitted was so low that we did not feel it justified an actual rating.

quotes & reviews

The quotes/reviews are taken directly from surveys submitted to us via our website (**www.lilaguide.com**). Other than spelling and minor grammatical changes, they come to you as they came to us. Quotes were selected based on how well they appeared to represent the collective opinions of the surveys submitted.

fact checking

We have contacted all of the businesses listed to verify their address and phone number, as well as to inquire about their hours, class schedules and web site information. Since some of this information may change after this guide has been printed, we appreciate you letting us know of any errors by notifying us via email at **lila@lilaguide.com**.

baby basics & accessories

City of Cleveland

Fairview Hospital

" ...this little hospital store was a total surprise... one of the best hospital gift shops I've been to... unique gift items for the last minute new baby visit... I wouldn't make a seperate trip, but you are sure to find something so that you don't arrive empty-handed... **"**

Furniture, Bedding & Decor	✗	$$$	Prices
Gear & Equipment	✗	❹	Product availability
Nursing & Feeding	✗	❹	Staff knowledge
Safety & Babycare	✗	❹	Customer service
Clothing, Shoes & Accessories	✗	❸	Decor
Books, Toys & Entertainment	✗		

WWW.FAIRVIEWHOSPITAL.ORG

CLEVELAND—18101 LORAIN AVE (AT VALLEY PKY); 216.476.7212; M-F 10-7, SA-SU 1-5

Payless Shoe Source

" ...a good place for deals on children's shoes... staff is helpful with sizing... the selection and prices for kids' shoes can't be beat, but the quality isn't always spectacular... good leather shoes for cheap... great variety of all sizes and widths... I get my son's shoes here and don't feel like I'm wasting my money since he'll outgrow them in 3 months anyway... **"**

Furniture, Bedding & Decor	✗	$$	Prices
Gear & Equipment	✗	❸	Product availability
Nursing & Feeding	✗	❸	Staff knowledge
Safety & Babycare	✗	❸	Customer service
Clothing, Shoes & Accessories	✓	❸	Decor
Books, Toys & Entertainment	✗		

WWW.PAYLESS.COM

CLEVELAND—10814 LORAIN AVE (AT W 106TH ST); 216.251.3374; M-SA 10-8, SU 10-6

CLEVELAND—11716 DETROIT AVE (AT W 117TH ST); 216.228.6150; M-SA 10-8, SU 11-5

CLEVELAND—230 W HURON RD (AT ONTARIO ST); 216.771.6569; M-SA 10-7, SU 12-6

CLEVELAND—3228 W 65TH ST (AT CLARK AVE); 216.631.3190; M-SA 10-8, SU 11-6

CLEVELAND—8069 EUCLID AVE (AT E 79TH ST); 216.421.1230; M-SA 9:30-8, SU 11-5

Rainbow Kids

" ...fun clothing styles for infants and tots at low prices... the quality isn't the same as the more expensive brands, but the sleepers and play outfits always hold up well... great place for basics... cute trendy shoe selection for your little walker... we love the prices... up-to-date selection... **"**

Furniture, Bedding & Decor	✗	$$	Prices
Gear & Equipment	✓	❸	Product availability
Nursing & Feeding	✗	❸	Staff knowledge
Safety & Babycare	✗	❸	Customer service
Clothing, Shoes & Accessories	✓	❸	Decor
Books, Toys & Entertainment	✓		

WWW.RAINBOWSHOPS.COM

CLEVELAND—1024 E 152ND ST (OFF ST CLAIR AVE); 216.249.3611; M-SA 10-6, SU 12-5

CLEVELAND—11331 BUCKEYE RD (AT E 116TH ST); 216.229.1407; M-SA 10-7, SU 12-5; PARKING LOT

CLEVELAND—RANDALL PARK MALL (AT WARRENSVILLE CTR RD); 216.581.9163; M-SA 10-9, SU 11-6; PARKING LOT

University Hospital.of Cleveland Atrium Gift Shop ★★★☆☆

❝...*the atrium gift shop offers many nice cards and small gifts that brighten people's days... Graco car seats are available here for just one dollar over cost... helpful, courteous staff... an easy stop on your way to the doctor's or to the hospital...* **❞**

Furniture, Bedding & Decor .... ✘	$$$ .... Prices
Gear & Equipment .... ✓	❹ .... Product availability
Nursing & Feeding .... ✘	❹ .... Staff knowledge
Safety & Babycare .... ✘	❹ .... Customer service
Clothing, Shoes & Accessories .... ✘	❹ .... Decor
Books, Toys & Entertainment .... ✓	

WWW.UHHS.COM

CLEVELAND—11100 EUCLID AVE (AT MAYFIELD RD); 216.844.1245; M 9-6, T 9-7:30, W 9-6, TH 9-7:30, F 9-6, SA 9-4:30, SU 11-4:30; PARKING LOT

Suburbs – East Side

★★★★★

"lila picks"

★Oh How Cute   ★Pottery Barn Kids

★Playground World

April Cornell

❝...beautiful, classic dresses and accessories for special occasions... I love the matching 'mommy and me' outfits... lots of fun knickknacks for sale... great selection of baby wear on their web site... rest assured your baby won't look like every other child in these adorable outfits... very frilly and girlie—beautiful... **❞**

Furniture, Bedding & Decor	✗	$$$...................................... Prices
Gear & Equipment	✗	❸ .... Product availability
Nursing & Feeding	✗	❹ .... Staff knowledge
Safety & Babycare	✗	❹ ....Customer service
Clothing, Shoes & Accessories	✓	❹ .... Decor
Books, Toys & Entertainment	✗	

WWW.APRILCORNELL.COM

LYNDHURST—24659 CEDAR RD (AT LEGACY VILLAGE); 216.382.7190; M-SA 10-9, SU 12-6

Baby Depot At Burlington
Coat Factory

❝...a large, 'super store' layout with a ton of baby gear... wide aisles, packed shelves, barely existent customer service and awesome prices... everything from bottles, car seats and strollers to gliders, cribs and clothes... I always find something worth getting... a little disorganized and hard to locate items you're looking for... the staff is not always knowledgeable about their merchandise... return policy is store credit only... **❞**

Furniture, Bedding & Decor	✓	$$.. Prices
Gear & Equipment	✓	❸ .... Product availability
Nursing & Feeding	✓	❸ .... Staff knowledge
Safety & Babycare	✓	❸ ....Customer service
Clothing, Shoes & Accessories	✓	❸ .... Decor
Books, Toys & Entertainment	✓	

WWW.BABYDEPOT.COM

NORTH RANDALL—20801 MILES RD (AT RANDALL PARK MALL); 216.587.1743; M-SA 10-9, SU 11-6; PARKING LOT

Baby Talk

Furniture, Bedding & Decor	✗	✗ .... Gear & Equipment
Nursing & Feeding	✗	✗ .... Safety & Babycare
Clothing, Shoes & Accessories	✓	✗ .... Books, Toys & Entertainment

NORTH RANDALL—4836 NORTHFIELD RD (AT MILES RD); 216.662.9900; M-F 10-8, SA 10-6, SU 12-5; PARKING LOT

BabyGap/GapKids ★★★★☆

"...colorful baby and toddler clothing in clean, well-lit stores... great return policy... it's the Gap, so you know what you're getting—colorful, cute and well-made clothing... best place for baby hats... prices are reasonable especially since there's always a sale of some sort going on... sales, sales, sales—frequent and fantastic... everything I'm looking for in infant clothing—snap crotches, snaps up the front, all natural fabrics and great styling... fun seasonal selections—a great place to shop for gifts as well as for your own kids... although it can get busy, staff generally seem accommodating and helpful..."

Furniture, Bedding & Decor	✗	$$$	Prices
Gear & Equipment	✗	❶	Product availability
Nursing & Feeding	✗	❹	Staff knowledge
Safety & Babycare	✗	❹	Customer service
Clothing, Shoes & Accessories	✓	❹	Decor
Books, Toys & Entertainment	✗		

WWW.GAP.COM

BEACHWOOD—26300 CEDAR RD (AT RICHMOND RD); 216.831.1178; M-F 10-9, SA 10-7:30, SU 12-6; PARKING LOT

Baci ★★★★☆

"...for the fashion forward mom and kid, this shop and web site has it all... bathing suits to dresses, infants to school age, boys and girls—all with a European flair... Chipie, Catimini, Lili Gaufrette... get ready to lay down some cash and make sure to check out the sales..."

Furniture, Bedding & Decor	✗	$$$$$	Prices
Gear & Equipment	✗	❸	Product availability
Nursing & Feeding	✗	❷	Staff knowledge
Safety & Babycare	✗	❷	Customer service
Clothing, Shoes & Accessories	✓	❹	Decor
Books, Toys & Entertainment	✗		

WWW.BACIKIDS.COM

BEACHWOOD—2101 RICHMOND RD (AT CEDAR RD); 216.896.1111

Bellini ★★★★☆

"...high-end furniture for a gorgeous nursery... if you're looking for the kind of furniture you see in magazines then this is the place to go... excellent quality... yes, it's pricey, but the quality is impeccable... free delivery and setup... their furniture is built to withstand the abuse my tots dish out... they sell very unique merchandise, ranging from cribs to bedding and even some clothes... our nursery design was inspired by their store decor... I wish they had more frequent sales..."

Furniture, Bedding & Decor	✓	$$$$	Prices
Gear & Equipment	✗	❹	Product availability
Nursing & Feeding	✗	❹	Staff knowledge
Safety & Babycare	✗	❹	Customer service
Clothing, Shoes & Accessories	✗	❹	Decor
Books, Toys & Entertainment	✓		

WWW.BELLINI.COM

BEACHWOOD—27820 CHAGRIN BLVD (AT IRVING PARK AVE); 216.765.1015; PARKING LOT

Bombay Kids ★★★★☆

"...the kids section of this furniture store carries out-of-the-ordinary items... whimsical, pastel grandfather clocks... zebra bean bags... perfect for my eclectic taste... I now prefer my daughter's room to my own... clean bathroom with changing area and wipes... they have a little table with crayons and coloring books for the kids... easy and relaxed shopping destination..."

Furniture, Bedding & Decor	✓	$$$	Prices

Gear & Equipment	✗	❹ .... Product availability
Nursing & Feeding	✗	❹ .... Staff knowledge
Safety & Babycare	✗	❹ .... Customer service
Clothing, Shoes & Accessories	✗	❹ .... Decor
Books, Toys & Entertainment	✗	

WWW.BOMBAYKIDS.COM

LYNDHURST—24675 CEDAR RD (AT LEGACY VILLAGE); 216.382.5805; M-SA
10-9, SU 11-5

Carter's ★★★★☆

❝...always a great selection of inexpensive baby basics—everything
from clothing to linens... I always find something at 'giveaway prices'
during one of their frequent sales... busy and crowded—it can be a
chaotic shopping experience... 30 to 50 percent less than what you
would pay at other boutiques... I bought five pieces of baby clothing
for less than $40... durable, adorable and affordable... most stores have
a small play area for kids in center of store so you can get your
shopping done... ❞

Furniture, Bedding & Decor	✓	$$.. Prices
Gear & Equipment	✗	❹ .... Product availability
Nursing & Feeding	✗	❹ .... Staff knowledge
Safety & Babycare	✗	❹ .... Customer service
Clothing, Shoes & Accessories	✓	❹ .... Decor
Books, Toys & Entertainment	✓	

WWW.CARTERS.COM

MAYFIELD HEIGHTS—1562 GOLDEN GATE PLZ (AT MAYFIELD RD);
440.684.9590; M-SA 10-8, SU 11-6; PARKING LOT

Children's Orchard ★★★⯪☆

❝...a friendly resale boutique... the clothes and gear are super clean
and sold at amazing prices... amazing prices on clothing that is hardly
used and practically brand new... shoes, toys, furniture, hair pretties,
crib sets, etc... fantastic deals on well-selected used items... prices are
great and you can pretty much always find something useful... a great
place to buy those everyday play outfits... a lot of name brands at
steeply discounted prices... ❞

Furniture, Bedding & Decor	✓	$$.. Prices
Gear & Equipment	✓	❸ .... Product availability
Nursing & Feeding	✓	❹ .... Staff knowledge
Safety & Babycare	✓	❹ .... Customer service
Clothing, Shoes & Accessories	✓	❸ .... Decor
Books, Toys & Entertainment	✓	

WWW.CHILDRENSORCHARD.COM

CHAGRIN FALLS—8440 E WASHINGTON ST (AT CHILLICOTHE RD);
440.543.4443; M-SA 10-6, SU 12-4; PARKING LOT

Children's Place, The ★★★⯪☆

❝...great bargains on cute clothing... shoes, socks, swimsuits,
sunglasses and everything in between... lots of '3 for $20' type deals on
sleepers, pants and mix-and-match separates... so much more
affordable than the other 'big chains'... don't expect the most unique
stuff here, but it wears and washes well... cheap clothing for cheap
prices... you can leave the store with bags full of clothes without
putting a huge dent in your wallet... ❞

Furniture, Bedding & Decor	✗	$$.. Prices
Gear & Equipment	✗	❹ .... Product availability
Nursing & Feeding	✗	❹ .... Staff knowledge
Safety & Babycare	✗	❹ .... Customer service
Clothing, Shoes & Accessories	✓	❹ .... Decor
Books, Toys & Entertainment	✓	

WWW.CHILDRENSPLACE.COM

BEACHWOOD—26300 CEDAR RD (AT RICHMOND RD); 216.360.9380; M-F 10-9, SA 10-7:30, SU 12-6; PARKING LOT

Costco ★★★⯪☆

"...*dependable place for bulk diapers, wipes and formula at discount prices... clothing selection is very hit-or-miss... avoid shopping there during nights and weekends if possible, because parking and checkout lines are brutal... they don't have a huge selection of brands, but the brands they do have are almost always in stock and at a great price... lowest prices around for diapers and formula... kid's clothing tends to be picked through, but it's worth looking for great deals on name-brand items like Carter's...* **"**

Furniture, Bedding & Decor .... ✓	$$ .... Prices
Gear & Equipment .... ✓	❸ .... Product availability
Nursing & Feeding .... ✓	❸ .... Staff knowledge
Safety & Babycare .... ✓	❸ .... Customer service
Clothing, Shoes & Accessories....... ✓	❷ .... Decor
Books, Toys & Entertainment .... ✓	

WWW.COSTCO.COM

MAYFIELD HEIGHTS—1409 GOLDEN GATE BLVD (AT MAYFIELD RD); 440.544.1350; M-F 11-8:30, SA 9:30-6, SU 10-6

Dillard's ★★★★☆

"...*this store has beautiful clothes, and if you catch a sale, you can get great quality clothes at super bargain prices... good customer service and helpful staff... a huge selection of merchandise for boys and girls... nice layette department... some furnishings like little tables and chairs... beautiful displays... the best part is that in addition to shopping for your kids, you can also shop for yourself...* **"**

Furniture, Bedding & Decor .... ✓	$$$ .... Prices
Gear & Equipment .... ✗	❹ .... Product availability
Nursing & Feeding .... ✗	❸ .... Staff knowledge
Safety & Babycare .... ✗	❹ .... Customer service
Clothing, Shoes & Accessories....... ✓	❹ .... Decor
Books, Toys & Entertainment .... ✓	

WWW.DILLARDS.COM

BEACHWOOD—26500 CEDAR RD (AT BEACHWOOLD PLACE MALL); 216.464.6000; M-SA 10-9, SU 12-6

EUCLID—1280 E 260TH ST (AT EUCLID SQ MALL); 216.289.8200; M-SA 11-7, SU 12-6

Gymboree ★★★★☆

"...*beautiful clothing and great quality... colorful and stylish baby and kids wear... lots of fun birthday gift ideas... easy exchange and return policy... items usually go on sale pretty quickly... save money with Gymbucks... many stores have a play area which makes shopping with my kids fun (let alone feasible)...* **"**

Furniture, Bedding & Decor .... ✗	$$$ .... Prices
Gear & Equipment .... ✗	❹ .... Product availability
Nursing & Feeding .... ✗	❹ .... Staff knowledge
Safety & Babycare .... ✗	❹ .... Customer service
Clothing, Shoes & Accessories....... ✓	❹ .... Decor
Books, Toys & Entertainment .... ✓	

WWW.GYMBOREE.COM

BEACHWOOD—26300 CEDAR RD (AT RICHMOND RD); 216.360.0031; M-F 10-9, SA 10-7, SU 12-6 ; PARKING LOT

Initially You Too Personalized

★★★★☆

"...this is a personalized gift store... shirts, burp clothes, blankets, cups, mirrors... unique gifts that you can't find anywhere else... whether I'm looking for a baby present or a graduation gift, if I want to spend $10 or $100, I'm always guaranteed to find something wonderful... one-stop shopping!.. I was impressed... **"**

Furniture, Bedding & Decor	✓	$$$	Prices
Gear & Equipment	✗	❹	Product availability
Nursing & Feeding	✓	❺	Staff knowledge
Safety & Babycare	✗	❹	Customer service
Clothing, Shoes & Accessories	✓	❹	Decor
Books, Toys & Entertainment	✓		

WWW.NAMES2U.COM

BEACHWOOD—27129 CHAGRIN BLVD (AT VILLAGE SQ); 216.831.0007; PARKING LOT

Janie And Jack

★★★★☆

"...gorgeous clothing and some accessories (shoes, socks, etc.)... fun to look at, somewhat pricey, but absolutely adorable clothes for little ones... boutique-like clothes at non-boutique prices—especially on sale... high-quality infant and toddler clothes anyone would love—always good for a baby gift... I always check the clearance racks in the back of the store... their decor is darling—a really fun shopping experience... **"**

Furniture, Bedding & Decor	✗	$$$$	Prices
Gear & Equipment	✓	❹	Product availability
Nursing & Feeding	✗	❹	Staff knowledge
Safety & Babycare	✗	❹	Customer service
Clothing, Shoes & Accessories	✓	❹	Decor
Books, Toys & Entertainment	✗		

WWW.JANIEANDJACK.COM

LYNDHURST—24655 CEDAR RD (AT RICHMOND RD); 216.691.0323; M-TH 10-8, F-SA 10-9, SU 12-6; PARKING LOT

JCPenney

★★★☆☆

"...always a good place to find clothes and other baby basics... the registry process was seamless... staff is generally friendly but the lines always seem long and slow... they don't have the greatest selection of toddler clothes, but their baby section is great... we had some damaged furniture delivered but customer service was easy and accommodating... a pretty limited selection of gear, but what they have is priced right... **"**

Furniture, Bedding & Decor	✓	$$	Prices
Gear & Equipment	✓	❸	Product availability
Nursing & Feeding	✓	❸	Staff knowledge
Safety & Babycare	✓	❸	Customer service
Clothing, Shoes & Accessories	✓	❸	Decor
Books, Toys & Entertainment	✓		

WWW.JCPENNEY.COM

RICHMOND HEIGHTS—701 RICHMOND RD (AT RICHMOND TOWN SQ); 440.449.3800; M-SA 10-9, SU 11-6; PARKING LOT

Joseph Beth Booksellers

★★★★☆

"...my favorite bookstore in the Cleveland area... fantastic selection of children's books and educational toys... great play space for kids!.. I go there with my son even when I don't need to buy anyting just so he can play with the train set and the puppets... all the resources you need in order to get ready for your baby's arrival... I love the cafe... **"**

Furniture, Bedding & Decor	✗	$$	Prices

Gear & Equipment	✗	❹ .... Product availability
Nursing & Feeding	✗	❹ .... Staff knowledge
Safety & Babycare	✗	❹ .... Customer service
Clothing, Shoes & Accessories	✗	❹ .... Decor
Books, Toys & Entertainment	✓	

WWW.JOSEPHBETH.COM

LYNDHURST—24519 CEDAR RD (AT LEGACY VLG); 216.691.7000; M-TH 9-10, F-SA 9-11, SU 10-8 ; PARKING LOT

Kate & Bud's Closet ★★★★★

"...cute personalized and decorated clothing... I like giving these items as shower gifts... my favorites are the big brother/big sister shirts for siblings... good quality and reasonable prices... this shop won't break the bank... "

Furniture, Bedding & Decor	✗	$$$ .... Prices
Gear & Equipment	✗	❸ .... Product availability
Nursing & Feeding	✗	❺ .... Staff knowledge
Safety & Babycare	✗	❺ .... Customer service
Clothing, Shoes & Accessories	✓	❹ .... Decor
Books, Toys & Entertainment	✗	

HIGHLAND HEIGHTS—422 LONGSPUR RD (AT TOURELLE RD); 440.473.1315; PARKING LOT

Kid's Foot Locker ★★★⯪☆

"...Nike, Reebok and Adidas for your little ones... hip, trendy and quite pricey... perfect for the sports addict dad who wants his kid sporting the latest NFL duds... shoes cost close to what the adult variety costs... generally good quality... they carry infant and toddler sizes... "

Furniture, Bedding & Decor	✗	$$$ .... Prices
Gear & Equipment	✗	❸ .... Product availability
Nursing & Feeding	✗	❸ .... Staff knowledge
Safety & Babycare	✗	❸ .... Customer service
Clothing, Shoes & Accessories	✓	❸ .... Decor
Books, Toys & Entertainment	✗	

WWW.KIDSFOOTLOCKER.COM

NORTH RANDALL—20801 MILES RD (AT RANDALL PARK MALL); 216.581.1542; M-SA 10-9, SU 12-6

RICHMOND HEIGHTS—691 RICHMOND RD (AT GERALDINE RD); 440.446.0923; M-SA 10-9, SU 11-6

Kohl's ★★★★☆

"...nice one-stop shopping for the whole family—everything from clothing to baby gear... great sales on clothing and a good selection of higher-end brands... stylish, inexpensive clothes for babies through 24 months... very easy shopping experience... dirt-cheap sales and clearance prices... nothing super fancy, but just right for those everyday romper outfits... Graco, Eddie Bauer and other well-known brands... "

Furniture, Bedding & Decor	✓	$$ .... Prices
Gear & Equipment	✓	❹ .... Product availability
Nursing & Feeding	✓	❸ .... Staff knowledge
Safety & Babycare	✓	❸ .... Customer service
Clothing, Shoes & Accessories	✓	❸ .... Decor
Books, Toys & Entertainment	✓	

WWW.KOHLS.COM

HIGHLAND HEIGHTS—6245 WILSON MILLS RD (OFF HWY 271); 440.442.6300; M-SA 8-10, SU 10-8; FREE PARKING

Macaroni ★★★⯪☆

"...adorable, high-end clothes and accessories... wonderful fabrics and designs... for parents who want their kids to dress as well as they do...

excellent quality, but comes at a price... the staff can be quite helpful... **"**

Furniture, Bedding & Decor	✗	$$$$	Prices
Gear & Equipment	✗	❸	Product availability
Nursing & Feeding	✗	❹	Staff knowledge
Safety & Babycare	✗	❹	Customer service
Clothing, Shoes & Accessories	✓	❹	Decor
Books, Toys & Entertainment	✗		

WOODMERE—28601 CHAGRIN BLVD (AT ROSELAWN RD); 216.831.1010; M-W F-SA 10-6, TH 10-8; PARKING LOT

Nordstrom ★★★★☆

"_...quality service and quality clothes... awesome kids shoe department—almost as good as the one for adults... free balloons in the children's shoe area as well as drawing tables... in addition to their own brand, they carry a very nice selection of other high-end baby clothing including Ralph Lauren, Robeez, etc... adorable baby clothes— they make great shower gifts... such a wonderful shopping experience—their lounge is perfect for breastfeeding and for changing diapers... well-rounded selection of baby basics as well as fancy clothes for special events..._ **"**

Furniture, Bedding & Decor	✓	$$$$	Prices
Gear & Equipment	✓	❹	Product availability
Nursing & Feeding	✗	❹	Staff knowledge
Safety & Babycare	✗	❹	Customer service
Clothing, Shoes & Accessories	✓	❹	Decor
Books, Toys & Entertainment	✓		

WWW.NORDSTROM.COM

BEACHWOOD—26200 CEDAR RD (AT RICHMOND RD); 216.378.2121; M-SA 10-9, SU 12-6

Oh How Cute ★★★★★

"_...absolutely adorable clothes, shoes, and gifts... the diaper cake is my standard new baby gift, looks great and totally useful... hip and comfortable maternity clothes... the outfits by 'tea' are my favorites... items you won't find in the mainstream... expensive, but fun to splurge... especially good for gift giving... you can find great stuff on the sale racks at the end of each season..._ **"**

Furniture, Bedding & Decor	✗	$$$$	Prices
Gear & Equipment	✓	❹	Product availability
Nursing & Feeding	✗	❹	Staff knowledge
Safety & Babycare	✗	❹	Customer service
Clothing, Shoes & Accessories	✓	❹	Decor
Books, Toys & Entertainment	✓		

WWW.OH-HOWCUTE.COM

BEACHWOOD—26300 CEDAR RD (AT BEACHWOOD PL MALL); 216.378.9015; M-F 10-9, SA 10-7:30, SU 12-6; PARKING LOT

Old Navy ★★★★☆

"_...hip and 'in' clothes for infants and tots... plenty of steals on clearance items... T-shirts and pants for $10 or less... busy, busy, busy—long lines, especially on weekends... nothing fancy and you won't mind when your kids get down and dirty in these clothes... easy to wash, decent quality... you can shop for your baby, your toddler, your teen and yourself all at the same time... clothes are especially affordable when you hit their sales (post-holiday sales are amazing!)..._ **"**

Furniture, Bedding & Decor	✗	$$	Prices
Gear & Equipment	✗	❹	Product availability
Nursing & Feeding	✗	❸	Staff knowledge
Safety & Babycare	✗	❸	Customer service

Clothing, Shoes & Accessories....... ✗   ❸ .... Decor
Books, Toys & Entertainment .... ✗

WWW.OLDNAVY.COM

MAYFIELD HEIGHTS—1533 GOLDEN GATE PLAZA (AT MAYFIELD RD);
440.442.9900; M-SA 9-10, SU 10-6; PARKING LOT

SOLON—6025 KRUSE DR (AT BAINBRIDGE RD); 440.519.0847; M-SA 9-9, SU
10-6; PARKING LOT

Oshkosh B'Gosh   ★★★★☆

"...cute, sturdy clothes for infants and toddlers... frequent sales make
their high-quality merchandise a lot more affordable... doesn't every
American kid have to get a pair of their overalls?.. great selection of
cute clothes for boys... you can't go wrong here—their clothing is fun
and worth the price... customer service is pretty hit-or-miss from store
to store... we always walk out of here with something fun and
colorful... **"**

Furniture, Bedding & Decor .... ✗ $$$ .... Prices
Gear & Equipment .... ✗   ❹ .... Product availability
Nursing & Feeding .... ✗   ❹ .... Staff knowledge
Safety & Babycare .... ✗   ❹ .... Customer service
Clothing, Shoes & Accessories....... ✓   ❹ .... Decor
Books, Toys & Entertainment .... ✗

WWW.OSHKOSHBGOSH.COM

LYNDHURST—25339 CEDAR RD (AT RICHMOND RD); 216.291.8893; M-TH10-
8, F-SA 10-9, SU 11-5; PARKING LOT

Playground World   ★★★★★

"...if you are looking for a playhouse or jungle gym, this is a good
place to start... they also have lots of other toys from stuffed animals to
trains... Brio and Gund... everything from kitchens to riding toys, fun
for toddler and up... lots of plastic... fair prices... **"**

Furniture, Bedding & Decor .... ✗ $$$$ .... Prices
Gear & Equipment .... ✗   ❹ .... Product availability
Nursing & Feeding .... ✗   ❹ .... Staff knowledge
Safety & Babycare .... ✗   ❹ .... Customer service
Clothing, Shoes & Accessories....... ✗   ❹ .... Decor
Books, Toys & Entertainment .... ✗

WWW.PGWORLD.COM

BEDFORD HEIGHTS—24206 AURORA RD (AT ROCKSIDE RD); 440.735.1188;
M-TU 10-6, W 10-5, TH-F 10-6, SA 10-4, SU 11-4; PARKING LOT

Pottery Barn Kids   ★★★★★

"...stylish furniture, rugs, rockers and much more... they've found the
right mix between quality and price... finally a company that stands
behind what they sell—their customer service is great... gorgeous baby
decor and furniture that will make your nursery to-die-for... the play
area is so much fun—my daughter never wants to leave... a beautiful
store with tons of ideas for setting up your nursery or kid's room...
bright colors and cute patterns with basics to mix and match... if you
see something in the catalog, but not in the store, just ask because they
often have it in the back... **"**

Furniture, Bedding & Decor .... ✓ $$$$ .... Prices
Gear & Equipment .... ✗   ❹ .... Product availability
Nursing & Feeding .... ✗   ❹ .... Staff knowledge
Safety & Babycare .... ✗   ❹ .... Customer service
Clothing, Shoes & Accessories....... ✗   ❺ .... Decor
Books, Toys & Entertainment .... ✓

WWW.POTTERYBARNKIDS.COM

BEACHWOOD—2101 RICHMOND RD (AT CEDAR RD); 216.765.0246; M-F 10-
8, SA 10-6, SU 12-5; PARKING LOT

Priceless Kids

"...cute kids clothes at discounted prices... especially helpful for the early months when babies grow quickly and you don't want to feel bad about stained clothing... a bare-bones shopping experience... THE place to get casual clothes—T-shirts, sweatpants, pajamas, etc... I wasn't crazy about the decor and the store is overcrowded with stuff, but I did find Stride-Rite shoes for $10 and sleepers for $1 each... every August they have a huge winter coat sale... name brand items at knock down prices..."

Furniture, Bedding & Decor	✗	$$	Prices
Gear & Equipment	✗	❸	Product availability
Nursing & Feeding	✗	❸	Staff knowledge
Safety & Babycare	✗	❸	Customer service
Clothing, Shoes & Accessories	✓	❸	Decor
Books, Toys & Entertainment	✗		

WWW.PRICELESSKIDS.COM

MAYFIELD HEIGHTS—6420 MAYFIELD RD (AT GOLDEN GATE MALL);
440.995.1919; M-SA 10-9, SU 12-5; PARKING LOT

Rainbow Kids

"...fun clothing styles for infants and tots at low prices... the quality isn't the same as the more expensive brands, but the sleepers and play outfits always hold up well... great place for basics... cute trendy shoe selection for your little walker... we love the prices... up-to-date selection..."

Furniture, Bedding & Decor	✗	$$	Prices
Gear & Equipment	✓	❸	Product availability
Nursing & Feeding	✗	❸	Staff knowledge
Safety & Babycare	✗	❸	Customer service
Clothing, Shoes & Accessories	✓	❸	Decor
Books, Toys & Entertainment	✓		

WWW.RAINBOWSHOPS.COM

HIGHLAND HILLS—4071 LEE RD (AT HARVARD AVE); 216.751.6356; M-SA 10-7, SU 12-5; PARKING LOT

MAPLE HEIGHTS—20750 LIBBY RD (AT WARRENSVILLE CTR RD);
216.587.4250; M-SA 10-9, SU 12-5; PARKING LOT

MAPLE HEIGHTS—20850 LIBBY RD (AT WARRENSVILLE CTR RD);
216.663.1292

Rainbow Shop

"...fun clothing styles for infants and tots at low prices... the quality isn't the same as the more expensive brands, but the sleepers and play outfits always hold up well... great place for basics... cute trendy shoe selection for your little walker... we love the prices... up-to-date selection..."

Furniture, Bedding & Decor	✗	$$$	Prices
Gear & Equipment	✗	❸	Product availability
Nursing & Feeding	✗	❸	Staff knowledge
Safety & Babycare	✗	❸	Customer service
Clothing, Shoes & Accessories	✗	❸	Decor
Books, Toys & Entertainment	✗		

EAST CLEVELAND—13520 1/2 EUCLID AVE (AT SUPERIOR AVE);
216.851.1119; M-SA 10-7, SU 12-5; PARKING LOT

Sears

"...a decent selection of clothes and basic baby equipment... check out the Kids Club program—it's a great way to save money... you go to Sears to save money, not to be pampered... the quality of their merchandise is better than Wal-Mart, but don't expect anything too

special or different... not much in terms of gear, but tons of well-priced baby and toddler clothing... **"**

Furniture, Bedding & Decor	✓	$$	Prices
Gear & Equipment	✓	❸	Product availability
Nursing & Feeding	✓	❸	Staff knowledge
Safety & Babycare	✓	❸	Customer service
Clothing, Shoes & Accessories	✓	❸	Decor
Books, Toys & Entertainment	✓		

WWW.SEARS.COM

NORTH RANDALL—501 RANDALL PARK MALL (AT RANDALL PARK MALL); 216.587.6300; M-F 10-9, SA 10-6, SU 11-5

RICHMOND HEIGHTS—621 RICHMOND RD (AT RICHMOND MALL); 440.473.8300; M-F 9-9, SA 10-6, SU 11-6

Sunbeam Shop For Children ★★★★☆

"...*a cute shop with even cuter clothes... toys and gifts too... the cool thing about this shop is the proceeds go to help people train for new jobs... run by cheerful volunteers... a little expensive, but they support a great social mission...* **"**

Furniture, Bedding & Decor	✗	$$$$	Prices
Gear & Equipment	✗	❸	Product availability
Nursing & Feeding	✗	❹	Staff knowledge
Safety & Babycare	✗	❹	Customer service
Clothing, Shoes & Accessories	✓	❹	Decor
Books, Toys & Entertainment	✓		

WWW.VGSJOB.ORG

CLEVELAND HEIGHTS—3469 FAIRMOUNT BLVD (AT S TAYLOR RD); 216.397.3929; M-F 10-5:30, SA 10-5; PARKING LOT

Talbots Kids ★★★⯪☆

"...*a nice alternative to the typical department store experience... expensive, but fantastic quality... great for holiday and special occasion outfits including christening outfits... well-priced, conservative children's clothing... cute selections for infants, toddlers and kids... sales are fantastic—up to half off at least a couple times a year... the best part is, you can also shop for yourself while shopping for baby...* **"**

Furniture, Bedding & Decor	✗	$$$$	Prices
Gear & Equipment	✗	❹	Product availability
Nursing & Feeding	✗	❹	Staff knowledge
Safety & Babycare	✗	❹	Customer service
Clothing, Shoes & Accessories	✓	❹	Decor
Books, Toys & Entertainment	✗		

WWW.TALBOTS.COM

LYNDHURST—25225 CEDAR RD (AT RICHMOND RD); 216.382.2576; M-TH 10-8, F-SA 10-9, SU 12-6

Target ★★★★☆

"...*our favorite place to shop for kids' stuff—good selection and very affordable... guilt-free shopping—kids grow so fast so I don't want to pay high department-store prices... everything from diapers and sippy cups to car seats and strollers... easy return policy... generally helpful staff, but you don't go for the service—you go for the prices... decent registry that won't freak your friends out with outrageous prices... easy, convenient shopping for well-priced items... all the big-box brands available—Graco, Evenflo, Eddie Bauer, etc....* **"**

Furniture, Bedding & Decor	✓	$$	Prices
Gear & Equipment	✓	❹	Product availability
Nursing & Feeding	✓	❸	Staff knowledge
Safety & Babycare	✓	❸	Customer service
Clothing, Shoes & Accessories	✓	❸	Decor

Books, Toys & Entertainment .... ✓

WWW.TARGET.COM

BEACHWOOD—14070 CEDAR RD (AT WARRENSVILLE CTR RD); 216.416.0025; M-SA 8-10, SU 8-9; PARKING LOT

BEDFORD—22735 ROCKSIDE RD (AT NORTHFIELD RD); 440.232.2093; M-SA 8-10, SU 8-9; PARKING LOT

MAYFIELD HEIGHTS—1285 SOM CTR RD (AT MAYFIELD RD); 440.995.9300; M-SA 8-10, SU 8-9; PARKING LOT

participate in our survey at

Suburbs – West Side

★★★★★

"lila picks"

★ Babies R Us ★ Lulu & Claire

Babies R Us ★★★★★

"...everything baby under one roof... they have a wide selection and carry most 'mainstream' items such as Graco, Fisher-Price, Avent and Britax... great customer service—given how big the stores are, I was pleasantly surprised at how attentive the staff was... easy return policy... super busy on weekends so try to visit on a weekday for the best service... keep an eye out for great coupons, deals and frequent sales... easy and comprehensive registry... shopping here is so easy—you've got to check it out... **"**

Furniture, Bedding & Decor	✓	$$$	Prices
Gear & Equipment	✓	❹	Product availability
Nursing & Feeding	✓	❹	Staff knowledge
Safety & Babycare	✓	❹	Customer service
Clothing, Shoes & Accessories	✓	❹	Decor
Books, Toys & Entertainment	✓		

WWW.BABIESRUS.COM

NORTH OLMSTED—26520 LORAIN RD (AT GREAT NORTHERN MALL); 440.716.8614; M-SA 9:30-9:30, SU 11-7; PARKING LOT

Baby Depot At Burlington Coat Factory ★★★½☆

"...a large, 'super store' layout with a ton of baby gear... wide aisles, packed shelves, barely existent customer service and awesome prices... everything from bottles, car seats and strollers to gliders, cribs and clothes... I always find something worth getting... a little disorganized and hard to locate items you're looking for... the staff is not always knowledgeable about their merchandise... return policy is store credit only... **"**

Furniture, Bedding & Decor	✓	$$	Prices
Gear & Equipment	✓	❸	Product availability
Nursing & Feeding	✓	❸	Staff knowledge
Safety & Babycare	✓	❸	Customer service
Clothing, Shoes & Accessories	✓	❸	Decor
Books, Toys & Entertainment	✓		

WWW.BABYDEPOT.COM

MIDDLEBURG HEIGHTS—6875 SOUTHLAND DR (AT W 130TH ST); 440.842.6808; M-SA 10-9, SU 11-6; PARKING LOT

BabyGap/GapKids ★★★★☆

"...colorful baby and toddler clothing in clean, well-lit stores... great return policy... it's the Gap, so you know what you're getting—colorful, cute and well-made clothing... best place for baby hats... prices are reasonable especially since there's always a sale of some sort going *on... sales, sales, sales—frequent and fantastic... everything I'm looking for in infant clothing—snap crotches, snaps up the front, all natural fabrics and great styling... fun seasonal selections—a great place to shop for gifts as well as for your own kids... although it can get busy, staff generally seem accommodating and helpful...* **"**

Furniture, Bedding & Decor	✗		$$$	Prices
Gear & Equipment	✗	❹		Product availability
Nursing & Feeding	✗	❹		Staff knowledge
Safety & Babycare	✗	❹		Customer service
Clothing, Shoes & Accessories	✓	❹		Decor
Books, Toys & Entertainment	✓			

WWW.GAP.COM

FAIRVIEW PARK—3145 WESTGATE MALL (AT WESTGATE MALL); 440.356.4722; M-SA 10-9, SU 11-7; MALL PARKING

STRONGSVILLE—820 SOUTHPARK CTR (AT ROYALTON RD); 440.846.8105; M-SA 10-9, SU 11-6; PARKING LOT

Bombay Kids

"*...the kids section of this furniture store carries out-of-the-ordinary items... whimsical, pastel grandfather clocks... zebra bean bags... perfect for my eclectic taste... I now prefer my daughter's room to my own... clean bathroom with changing area and wipes... they have a little table with crayons and coloring books for the kids... easy and relaxed shopping destination...* **"**

Furniture, Bedding & Decor	✓		$$$	Prices
Gear & Equipment	✗	❹		Product availability
Nursing & Feeding	✗	❹		Staff knowledge
Safety & Babycare	✗	❹		Customer service
Clothing, Shoes & Accessories	✗	❹		Decor
Books, Toys & Entertainment	✗			

WWW.BOMBAYKIDS.COM

WESTLAKE—30045 DETROIT RD (AT CROCKER RD); 440.249.5030; M-SA 10-9, SU 11-6

Children's Place, The

"*...great bargains on cute clothing... shoes, socks, swimsuits, sunglasses and everything in between... lots of '3 for $20' type deals on sleepers, pants and mix-and-match separates... so much more affordable than the other 'big chains'... don't expect the most unique stuff here, but it wears and washes well... cheap clothing for cheap prices... you can leave the store with bags full of clothes without putting a huge dent in your wallet...* **"**

Furniture, Bedding & Decor	✗		$$	Prices
Gear & Equipment	✗	❹		Product availability
Nursing & Feeding	✗	❹		Staff knowledge
Safety & Babycare	✗	❹		Customer service
Clothing, Shoes & Accessories	✓	❹		Decor
Books, Toys & Entertainment	✓			

WWW.CHILDRENSPLACE.COM

NORTH OLMSTED—190 GREAT NORTHERN MALL (AT GREAT NORTHERN BLVD); 440.686.0486; M-SA 10-9, SU 11-6; PARKING LOT

PARMA—7933 W RIDGEWOOD DR (AT RIDGE RD); 440.888.2165; M-SA 10-9, SU 11-6; PARKING LOT

STRONGSVILLE—500 SOUTHPARK CTR (AT ROYALTON RD); 440.878.9295; M-SA 10-9, SU 11-6; PARKING LOT

Children's Treasures Resale

"*...small resale shop... Monday they have extra discounts on their clothes and gear... I thought the selection could have been better to*

eliminate some of the clutter and overly worn items... a great way to save money on basic run around play clothes... **"**

Furniture, Bedding & Decor	✗	$$	Prices
Gear & Equipment	✗	❸	Product availability
Nursing & Feeding	✗	❸	Staff knowledge
Safety & Babycare	✗	❸	Customer service
Clothing, Shoes & Accessories	✓	❷	Decor
Books, Toys & Entertainment	✓		

LAKEWOOD—17415 DETROIT AVE (AT LARCHMONT AVE); 216.227.5683; M-F 2-6:30, SA 1-6:30; PARKING LOT

Closets Consignment Boutique

 ★★★☆☆

"...consignment shopping in a pleasant shop... great place to buy and sell... you get 50 percent of the selling price minus a handling fee... they will even donate your items to charity for you if they don't sell which eliminates the pickup hassle... hit or miss, but I almost always find something... all items in like new condition...** **"**

Furniture, Bedding & Decor	✗	$$	Prices
Gear & Equipment	✗	❸	Product availability
Nursing & Feeding	✗	❸	Staff knowledge
Safety & Babycare	✗	❸	Customer service
Clothing, Shoes & Accessories	✓	❸	Decor
Books, Toys & Entertainment	✗		

WWW.CLOSETSCONSIGNMENT.COM

ROCKY RIVER—1100 LINDA ST (AT LAKE RD); 440.333.5379; M-T F-SA 11-5, W-TH 11-8, SU 2-5; PARKING LOT

Dillard's

 ★★★★☆

"...this store has beautiful clothes, and if you catch a sale, you can get great quality clothes at super bargain prices... good customer service and helpful staff... a huge selection of merchandise for boys and girls... nice layette department... some furnishings like little tables and chairs... beautiful displays... the best part is that in addition to shopping for your kids, you can also shop for yourself...** **"**

Furniture, Bedding & Decor	✓	$$$	Prices
Gear & Equipment	✗	❹	Product availability
Nursing & Feeding	✗	❸	Staff knowledge
Safety & Babycare	✗	❹	Customer service
Clothing, Shoes & Accessories	✓	❹	Decor
Books, Toys & Entertainment	✓		

WWW.DILLARDS.COM

STRONGSVILLE—16996 SOUTHPARK CTR (AT ROYALTON RD); 440.846.8718; M-SA 10-9, SU 12-6

Gymboree

 ★★★★☆

"...beautiful clothing and great quality... colorful and stylish baby and kids wear... lots of fun birthday gift ideas... easy exchange and return policy... items usually go on sale pretty quickly... save money with Gymbucks... many stores have a play area which makes shopping with my kids fun (let alone feasible)...** **"**

Furniture, Bedding & Decor	✗	$$$	Prices
Gear & Equipment	✗	❹	Product availability
Nursing & Feeding	✗	❹	Staff knowledge
Safety & Babycare	✗	❹	Customer service
Clothing, Shoes & Accessories	✓	❹	Decor
Books, Toys & Entertainment	✓		

WWW.GYMBOREE.COM

NORTH OLMSTED—806 GREAT NORTHERN MALL (AT GREAT NORTHERN BLVD); 440.734.3066; M-SA 10-9, SU 11-6; PARKING LOT

STRONGSVILLE—17177 ROYALTON RD (AT HOWE RD); 440.846.9950; M-SA 10-9, SU 11-6; PARKING LOT

JCPenney

"..._always a good place to find clothes and other baby basics... the registry process was seamless... staff is generally friendly but the lines always seem long and slow... they don't have the greatest selection of toddler clothes, but their baby section is great... we had some damaged furniture delivered but customer service was easy and accommodating... a pretty limited selection of gear, but what they have is priced right..._ "

Furniture, Bedding & Decor	✓	$$	Prices
Gear & Equipment	✓	❸	Product availability
Nursing & Feeding	✓	❸	Staff knowledge
Safety & Babycare	✓	❸	Customer service
Clothing, Shoes & Accessories	✓	❸	Decor
Books, Toys & Entertainment	✓		

WWW.JCPENNEY.COM

NORTH OLMSTED—5100 GREAT NORTHERN BLVD (AT GREAT NORTHERN MALL); 440.779.8800; M-SA 10-9, SU 11-6; PARKING LOT

PARMA—7900 DAY DR (AT RIDGE RD); 440.845.7200; M-SA 10-9, SU 11:30-5:30; PARKING LOT

STRONGSVILLE—17177 ROYALTON RD (AT HOWE RD); 440.846.8419; M-SA 10-9, SU 11-6; PARKING LOT

Kohl's

"..._nice one-stop shopping for the whole family—everything from clothing to baby gear... great sales on clothing and a good selection of higher-end brands... stylish, inexpensive clothes for babies through 24 months... very easy shopping experience... dirt-cheap sales and clearance prices... nothing super fancy, but just right for those everyday romper outfits... Graco, Eddie Bauer and other well-known brands..._ "

Furniture, Bedding & Decor	✓	$$	Prices
Gear & Equipment	✓	❹	Product availability
Nursing & Feeding	✓	❸	Staff knowledge
Safety & Babycare	✓	❸	Customer service
Clothing, Shoes & Accessories	✓	❸	Decor
Books, Toys & Entertainment	✓		

WWW.KOHLS.COM

FAIRVIEW PARK—3221 WESTGATE MALL (AT W 210TH ST); 440.356.1500; M-SA 8-10, SU 10-8; FREE PARKING

PARMA—6860 RIDGE RD (AT DAY DR); 440.884.2600; M-SA 8-10, SU 10-8; FREE PARKING

STRONGSVILLE—17555 SOUTHPARK CTR (AT ROYALTON RD); 440.572.4474; M-SA 8-10, SU 10-8; FREE PARKING

Lulu & Claire

"..._the place to go for upscale babies and kids clothes... high-quality items... special gifts including hip and funky clothes... more for girls than boys... Baby Nay, Due Sorelle, Catamini... they carry the super high-end Bratt Decor furniture line...._ "

Furniture, Bedding & Decor	✓	$$$$	Prices
Gear & Equipment	✓	❹	Product availability
Nursing & Feeding	✗	❹	Staff knowledge
Safety & Babycare	✗	❹	Customer service
Clothing, Shoes & Accessories	✓	❺	Decor
Books, Toys & Entertainment	✗		

WWW.LULUANDCLAIRE.COM

ROCKY RIVER—2226 WOOSTER RD (AT RIVERWOOD AVE); 440.895.5858; T-TH 10:30-6, F 10:30-4, SA 11-4; PARKING LOT

Neverending Child ★★★☆☆

❝...resale shop... lots of bargains... went here after recovering from sticker shock at Old Navy... found a pair of like new jeans for my 9-month-old for $5!.. store clerk was preoccupied and didn't talk much, but I loved the bargain anyway... everything from clothes to furniture...**❞**

Furniture, Bedding & Decor	✓	$$ .... Prices
Gear & Equipment	✗	❹ .... Product availability
Nursing & Feeding	✗	❸ .... Staff knowledge
Safety & Babycare	✗	❸ .... Customer service
Clothing, Shoes & Accessories	✓	❷ .... Decor
Books, Toys & Entertainment	✓	

STRONGSVILLE—12245 PEARL RD (AT FALLING WATER RD); 440.572.3002; M-SA 10:15-5

Old Navy ★★★★☆

❝...hip and 'in' clothes for infants and tots... plenty of steals on clearance items... T-shirts and pants for $10 or less... busy, busy, busy—long lines, especially on weekends... nothing fancy and you won't mind when your kids get down and dirty in these clothes... easy to wash, decent quality... you can shop for your baby, your toddler, your teen and yourself all at the same time... clothes are especially affordable when you hit their sales (post-holiday sales are amazing!)...**❞**

Furniture, Bedding & Decor	✗	$$ .... Prices
Gear & Equipment	✗	❹ .... Product availability
Nursing & Feeding	✗	❸ .... Staff knowledge
Safety & Babycare	✗	❸ .... Customer service
Clothing, Shoes & Accessories	✓	❸ .... Decor
Books, Toys & Entertainment	✗	

WWW.OLDNAVY.COM

STRONGSVILLE—18260 ROYALTON RD (AT PEARL RD); 440.846.1890; M-SA 9-9, SU 11-6; PARKING LOT

Once Upon A Child ★★★★☆

❝...new and used items... the place for bargain baby items in like-new condition... a great bargain spot with a wide variety of clothes for baby... some inexpensive furniture... good selection, staff and prices... cluttered and hard to get through the store with kids... good toys and gear... some items are definitely more than 'gently used'... a kid's play area... good end-of-season sales... expect to sort through items... cash for your old items...**❞**

Furniture, Bedding & Decor	✓	$$ .... Prices
Gear & Equipment	✓	❸ .... Product availability
Nursing & Feeding	✗	❹ .... Staff knowledge
Safety & Babycare	✗	❹ .... Customer service
Clothing, Shoes & Accessories	✓	❸ .... Decor
Books, Toys & Entertainment	✓	

WWW.OUAC.COM

WESTLAKE—25028 CTR RIDGE RD (AT KING JAMES PKY); 440.899.1100; M-SA 10-6, SU 12-5; PARKING LOT

Once Upon A Time ★★★★☆

❝...terrific resale shop with one of a kind toys... great for Christmas stocking stuffers... great selection of adorable, gently worn clothing at reasonable prices... cool handmade wooden toys and educational toys...**❞**

Furniture, Bedding & Decor	✗	$$$ .... Prices
Gear & Equipment	✗	❸ .... Product availability
Nursing & Feeding	✗	❹ .... Staff knowledge

Safety & Babycare	✗	❹	Customer service
Clothing, Shoes & Accessories	✗	❹	Decor
Books, Toys & Entertainment	✗		

ROCKY RIVER—19285 DETROIT RD (AT WRIGHT AVE); 440.333.2327; T-F 10-7, M SA 10-5, SU 12-5; PARKING LOT

Priceless Kids ★★★⯪☆

❝...cute kids clothes at discounted prices... especially helpful for the early months when babies grow quickly and you don't want to feel bad about stained clothing... a bare-bones shopping experience... THE place to get casual clothes—T-shirts, sweatpants, pajamas, etc... I wasn't crazy about the decor and the store is overcrowded with stuff, but I did find Stride-Rite shoes for $10 and sleepers for $1 each... every August they have a huge winter coat sale... name brand items at knock down prices... **❞**

Furniture, Bedding & Decor	✗	$$	Prices
Gear & Equipment	✗	❸	Product availability
Nursing & Feeding	✗	❸	Staff knowledge
Safety & Babycare	✗	❸	Customer service
Clothing, Shoes & Accessories	✗	❸	Decor
Books, Toys & Entertainment	✗		

WWW.PRICELESSKIDS.COM

BROOKLYN—4816 RIDGE RD (AT RIDGE PARK SQ); 216.398.8240; M-SA 10-9, SU 12-5; PARKING LOT

Sears ★★★☆☆

❝...a decent selection of clothes and basic baby equipment... check out the Kids Club program—it's a great way to save money... you go to Sears to save money, not to be pampered... the quality of their merchandise is better than Wal-Mart, but don't expect anything too special or different... not much in terms of gear, but tons of well-priced baby and toddler clothing... **❞**

Furniture, Bedding & Decor	✓	$$	Prices
Gear & Equipment	✓	❸	Product availability
Nursing & Feeding	✓	❸	Staff knowledge
Safety & Babycare	✓	❸	Customer service
Clothing, Shoes & Accessories	✓	❸	Decor
Books, Toys & Entertainment	✓		

WWW.SEARS.COM

MIDDLEBURG HEIGHTS—6950 W 130TH ST (AT SOUTHLAND SHOPPING CTR); 440.886.7500; M-F 10-9, SA 8-9, SU 11-5

NORTH OLMSTED—5000 GREAT NORTHERN MALL (AT GREAT NORTHERN MALL); 440.777.8070; M-SA 10-9, SU 11-5

STRONGSVILLE—17271 SOUTHPARK CTR (AT SOUTH PARK CTR); 440.846.3500; M-SA 10-9, SU 11-5

Talbots Kids ★★★⯪☆

❝...a nice alternative to the typical department store experience... expensive, but fantastic quality... great for holiday and special occasion outfits including christening outfits... well-priced, conservative children's clothing... cute selections for infants, toddlers and kids... sales are fantastic—up to half off at least a couple times a year... the best part is, you can also shop for yourself while shopping for baby... **❞**

Furniture, Bedding & Decor	✗	$$$$	Prices
Gear & Equipment	✗	❹	Product availability
Nursing & Feeding	✗	❹	Staff knowledge
Safety & Babycare	✗	❹	Customer service
Clothing, Shoes & Accessories	✓	❹	Decor
Books, Toys & Entertainment	✗		

WWW.TALBOTS.COM

participate in our survey at

Target ★★★★☆

"...*our favorite place to shop for kids' stuff—good selection and very affordable... guilt-free shopping—kids grow so fast so I don't want to pay high department-store prices... everything from diapers and sippy cups to car seats and strollers... easy return policy... generally helpful staff, but you don't go for the service—you go for the prices... decent registry that won't freak your friends out with outrageous prices... easy, convenient shopping for well-priced items... all the big-box brands available—Graco, Evenflo, Eddie Bauer, etc....* **"**

Furniture, Bedding & Decor	✓	$$ .... Prices
Gear & Equipment	✓	❹ .... Product availability
Nursing & Feeding	✓	❸ .... Staff knowledge
Safety & Babycare	✓	❸ .... Customer service
Clothing, Shoes & Accessories	✓	❸ .... Decor
Books, Toys & Entertainment	✓	

WWW.TARGET.COM

PARMA—6850 RIDGE RD (AT DAY DR); 440.842.9001; M-SA 8-10, SU 8-9; PARKING LOT

ROCKY RIVER—20001 CTR RIDGE RD (AT HAMPTON RD); 440.895.2600; M-SA 8-10, SU 8-9; PARKING LOT

STRONGSVILLE—18200 ROYALTON RD (AT PEARL RD); 440.238.9924; M-SA 8-10, SU 8-9; PARKING LOT

USA Baby ★★★☆☆

"...*they carry an extensive selection of high-end nursery products such as furniture, bedding, accessories and highchairs... popular place to do all the shopping for your nursery... the staff knows their products well and can help you sort through their vast selection... allow plenty of time for your products to arrive, especially the big-ticket items (they offer loaners while you wait for your order to arrive)... they have great sales a few times a year and will match competitor prices... good selection, especially if you're getting ready to set up your nursery...* **"**

Furniture, Bedding & Decor	✓	$$$$ .... Prices
Gear & Equipment	✓	❹ .... Product availability
Nursing & Feeding	✓	❹ .... Staff knowledge
Safety & Babycare	✓	❹ .... Customer service
Clothing, Shoes & Accessories	✗	❹ .... Decor
Books, Toys & Entertainment	✓	

WWW.USABABY.COM

WESTLAKE—25027 CENTER RIDGE RD (AT KING JAMES PKWY); 440.835.9696; M-T TH 10-8, W F-SA 10-6, SU 12-5; PARKING LOT

Lake & Geauga

★★★★★
"lila picks"

- ★ Babies R Us
- ★ Bergs Baby & Teen Furniture
- ★ Playground World

Babies R Us ★★★★★

"...everything baby under one roof... they have a wide selection and carry most 'mainstream' items such as Graco, Fisher-Price, Avent and Britax... great customer service—given how big the stores are, I was pleasantly surprised at how attentive the staff was... easy return policy... super busy on weekends so try to visit on a weekday for the best service... keep an eye out for great coupons, deals and frequent sales... easy and comprehensive registry... shopping here is so easy—you've got to check it out... **"**

Furniture, Bedding & Decor	✓	$$$	Prices
Gear & Equipment	✓	❹	Product availability
Nursing & Feeding	✓	❹	Staff knowledge
Safety & Babycare	✓	❹	Customer service
Clothing, Shoes & Accessories	✓	❹	Decor
Books, Toys & Entertainment	✓		

WWW.BABIESRUS.COM

MENTOR—7841 MENTOR AVE (AT MENTOR CITY SHOPPING CTR); 440.974.7388; M-SA 9:30-9:30, SU 11-7; PARKING LOT

Baby Depot At Burlington
Coat Factory ★★★⯪☆

"...a large, 'super store' layout with a ton of baby gear... wide aisles, packed shelves, barely existent customer service and awesome prices... everything from bottles, car seats and strollers to gliders, cribs and clothes... I always find something worth getting... a little disorganized and hard to locate items you're looking for... the staff is not always knowledgeable about their merchandise... return policy is store credit only... **"**

Furniture, Bedding & Decor	✓	$$	Prices
Gear & Equipment	✓	❸	Product availability
Nursing & Feeding	✓	❸	Staff knowledge
Safety & Babycare	✓	❸	Customer service
Clothing, Shoes & Accessories	✓	❸	Decor
Books, Toys & Entertainment	✓		

WWW.BABYDEPOT.COM

MENTOR—7980 PLAZA BLVD (AT ROUTE 20); 440.255.4077; M-SA 10-9, SU 11-6; PARKING LOT

participate in our survey at

BabyGap/GapKids ★★★★☆

"...colorful baby and toddler clothing in clean, well-lit stores... great return policy... it's the Gap, so you know what you're getting—colorful, cute and well-made clothing... best place for baby hats... prices are reasonable especially since there's always a sale of some sort going on... sales, sales, sales—frequent and fantastic... everything I'm looking for in infant clothing—snap crotches, snaps up the front, all natural fabrics and great styling... fun seasonal selections—a great place to shop for gifts as well as for your own kids... although it can get busy, staff generally seem accommodating and helpful..."

Furniture, Bedding & Decor	✗	$$$	Prices
Gear & Equipment	✗	❹	Product availability
Nursing & Feeding	✗	❹	Staff knowledge
Safety & Babycare	✗	❹	Customer service
Clothing, Shoes & Accessories	✓	❹	Decor
Books, Toys & Entertainment	✓		

WWW.GAP.COM

MENTOR—7850 MENTOR AVE (AT PLAZA BLVD); 440.255.9776; M-SA 10-9 SU 11-6; PARKING LOT

Bergs Baby & Teen Furniture ★★★★★

"...a must-stop for any parent to be... high-quality, top notch furniture and baby gear... the most knowledgeable staff in all of Cleveland... they came to my house, set up, and fully assembled our crib and changing table—it couldn't have been easier... they can order items in custom colors and designs... reasonable prices with superb service..."

Furniture, Bedding & Decor	✓	$$$$	Prices
Gear & Equipment	✓	❺	Product availability
Nursing & Feeding	✓	❺	Staff knowledge
Safety & Babycare	✗	❺	Customer service
Clothing, Shoes & Accessories	✗	❺	Decor
Books, Toys & Entertainment	✓		

WWW.BERGSBABY.COM

WILLOUGHBY HILLS—27565 CHARDON RD (AT BISHOP RD); 440.585.2374; M TH 10-8, T-W F-SA 10-6; PARKING LOT

Children's Place, The ★★★½☆

"...great bargains on cute clothing... shoes, socks, swimsuits, sunglasses and everything in between... lots of '3 for $20' type deals on sleepers, pants and mix-and-match separates... so much more affordable than the other 'big chains'... don't expect the most unique stuff here, but it wears and washes well... cheap clothing for cheap prices... you can leave the store with bags full of clothes without putting a huge dent in your wallet..."

Furniture, Bedding & Decor	✗	$$	Prices
Gear & Equipment	✗	❹	Product availability
Nursing & Feeding	✗	❹	Staff knowledge
Safety & Babycare	✗	❹	Customer service
Clothing, Shoes & Accessories	✓	❹	Decor
Books, Toys & Entertainment	✓		

WWW.CHILDRENSPLACE.COM

MENTOR—7850 MENTOR AVE (BTWN RT 615 AND 306); 440.205.0890; M-SA 10-9, SU 11-6; PARKING LOT

Dillard's ★★★★☆

"...this store has beautiful clothes, and if you catch a sale, you can get great quality clothes at super bargain prices... good customer service and helpful staff... a huge selection of merchandise for boys and girls... nice layette department... some furnishings like little tables and chairs...

beautiful displays... the best part is that in addition to shopping for your kids, you can also shop for yourself... **"**

Furniture, Bedding & Decor	✓	$$$	Prices
Gear & Equipment	✗	❹	Product availability
Nursing & Feeding	✗	❸	Staff knowledge
Safety & Babycare	✗	❹	Customer service
Clothing, Shoes & Accessories	✓	❹	Decor
Books, Toys & Entertainment	✓		

WWW.DILLARDS.COM

MENTOR—7850 MENTOR AVE (AT GREAT LAKE MALL); 440.255.5651; M-SA 10-9, SU 12-6

Gymboree ★★★★☆

"*...beautiful clothing and great quality... colorful and stylish baby and kids wear... lots of fun birthday gift ideas... easy exchange and return policy... items usually go on sale pretty quickly... save money with Gymbucks... many stores have a play area which makes shopping with my kids fun (let alone feasible)...* **"**

Furniture, Bedding & Decor	✗	$$$	Prices
Gear & Equipment	✗	❹	Product availability
Nursing & Feeding	✗	❹	Staff knowledge
Safety & Babycare	✗	❹	Customer service
Clothing, Shoes & Accessories	✓	❹	Decor
Books, Toys & Entertainment	✓		

WWW.GYMBOREE.COM

MENTOR—7850 MENTOR AVE (AT GREAT LAKE MALL); 440.205.0102; FREE PARKING

JCPenney ★★★⯪☆

"*...always a good place to find clothes and other baby basics... the registry process was seamless... staff is generally friendly but the lines always seem long and slow... they don't have the greatest selection of toddler clothes, but their baby section is great... we had some damaged furniture delivered but customer service was easy and accommodating... a pretty limited selection of gear, but what they have is priced right...* **"**

Furniture, Bedding & Decor	✓	$$	Prices
Gear & Equipment	✓	❸	Product availability
Nursing & Feeding	✓	❸	Staff knowledge
Safety & Babycare	✓	❸	Customer service
Clothing, Shoes & Accessories	✓	❸	Decor
Books, Toys & Entertainment	✓		

WWW.JCPENNEY.COM

MENTOR—7850 MENTOR AVE (AT GREAT LAKE MALL); 440.255.4461; M-TH 10-9, F 9-10, SA 8-10, SU 11-8

Kohl's ★★★★☆

"*...nice one-stop shopping for the whole family—everything from clothing to baby gear... great sales on clothing and a good selection of higher-end brands... stylish, inexpensive clothes for babies through 24 months... very easy shopping experience... dirt-cheap sales and clearance prices... nothing super fancy, but just right for those everyday romper outfits... Graco, Eddie Bauer and other well-known brands...* **"**

Furniture, Bedding & Decor	✓	$$	Prices
Gear & Equipment	✓	❹	Product availability
Nursing & Feeding	✓	❸	Staff knowledge
Safety & Babycare	✓	❸	Customer service
Clothing, Shoes & Accessories	✓	❸	Decor
Books, Toys & Entertainment	✓		

WWW.KOHLS.COM

participate in our survey at

MENTOR—9581 MENTOR AVE (AT OLD JOHNNYCAKE); 440.354.5800; M-SA 8-10, SU 10-8; FREE PARKING

Old Navy ★★★★☆

❝...*hip and 'in' clothes for infants and tots... plenty of steals on clearance items... T-shirts and pants for $10 or less... busy, busy, busy—long lines, especially on weekends... nothing fancy and you won't mind when your kids get down and dirty in these clothes... easy to wash, decent quality... you can shop for your baby, your toddler, your teen and yourself all at the same time... clothes are especially affordable when you hit their sales (post-holiday sales are amazing!)...* **❞**

Furniture, Bedding & Decor	✗	$$	Prices
Gear & Equipment	✗	❹	Product availability
Nursing & Feeding	✗	❸	Staff knowledge
Safety & Babycare	✗	❸	Customer service
Clothing, Shoes & Accessories	✓	❸	Decor
Books, Toys & Entertainment	✗		

WWW.OLDNAVY.COM

MENTOR—7317 MENTOR AVE (AT MIDLAND RD); 440.942.7577; M-SA 9-9, SU 10-6

Once Upon A Child ★★★★☆

❝...*new and used items... the place for bargain baby items in like-new condition... a great bargain spot with a wide variety of clothes for baby... some inexpensive furniture... good selection, staff and prices... cluttered and hard to get through the store with kids... good toys and gear... some items are definitely more than 'gently used'... a kid's play area... good end-of-season sales... expect to sort through items... cash for your old items...* **❞**

Furniture, Bedding & Decor	✓	$$	Prices
Gear & Equipment	✓	❸	Product availability
Nursing & Feeding	✗	❹	Staff knowledge
Safety & Babycare	✗	❹	Customer service
Clothing, Shoes & Accessories	✓	❸	Decor
Books, Toys & Entertainment	✓		

WWW.OUAC.COM

MENTOR—7537 MENTOR AVE (AT ROUTE 306); 440.951.7222; PARKING LOT

Playground World ★★★★★

❝...*if you are looking for a playhouse or jungle gym, this is a good place to start... they also have lots of other toys from stuffed animals to trains... Brio and Gund... everything from kitchens to riding toys, fun for toddler and up... lots of plastic... fair prices...* **❞**

Furniture, Bedding & Decor	✗	$$$$	Prices
Gear & Equipment	✗	❹	Product availability
Nursing & Feeding	✗	❹	Staff knowledge
Safety & Babycare	✗	❹	Customer service
Clothing, Shoes & Accessories	✗	❹	Decor
Books, Toys & Entertainment	✓		

WWW.PGWORLD.COM

CHESTERLAND—8035 MAYFIELD RD (AT HAROLD DR); 440.729.0909; M-F 10-6, SA 10-5, SU 11-5; PARKING LOT

Sears ★★★☆☆

❝...*a decent selection of clothes and basic baby equipment... check out the Kids Club program—it's a great way to save money... you go to Sears to save money, not to be pampered... the quality of their merchandise is better than Wal-Mart, but don't expect anything too special or different... not much in terms of gear, but tons of well-priced baby and toddler clothing...* **❞**

Furniture, Bedding & Decor	✓	$$	Prices
Gear & Equipment	✓	❸	Product availability
Nursing & Feeding	✓	❸	Staff knowledge
Safety & Babycare	✓	❸	Customer service
Clothing, Shoes & Accessories	✓	❸	Decor
Books, Toys & Entertainment	✓		

WWW.SEARS.COM

MENTOR—7875 JOHNNYCAKE RIDGE RD (AT DEEPWOOD BLVD);
440.974.5500; M-F 10-9, SA 8-9, SU 11-6

Target ★★★★☆

"...our favorite place to shop for kids' stuff—good selection and very affordable... guilt-free shopping—kids grow so fast so I don't want to pay high department-store prices... everything from diapers and sippy cups to car seats and strollers... easy return policy... generally helpful staff, but you don't go for the service—you go for the prices... decent registry that won't freak your friends out with outrageous prices... easy, convenient shopping for well-priced items... all the big-box brands available—Graco, Evenflo, Eddie Bauer, etc...."

Furniture, Bedding & Decor	✓	$$	Prices
Gear & Equipment	✓	❹	Product availability
Nursing & Feeding	✓	❸	Staff knowledge
Safety & Babycare	✓	❸	Customer service
Clothing, Shoes & Accessories	✓	❸	Decor
Books, Toys & Entertainment	✓		

WWW.TARGET.COM

WILLOUGHBY—440.975.1922; M-SA 8-10, SU 8-9; PARKING LOT

Lorain & Medina

"lila picks"

★ Playground World

Children's Orchard ★★★½☆

"...a friendly resale boutique... the clothes and gear are super clean and sold at amazing prices... amazing prices on clothing that is hardly used and practically brand new... shoes, toys, furniture, hair pretties, crib sets, etc... fantastic deals on well-selected used items... prices are great and you can pretty much always find something useful... a great place to buy those everyday play outfits... a lot of name brands at steeply discounted prices..."

Furniture, Bedding & Decor	✓	$$	Prices
Gear & Equipment	✓	❸	Product availability
Nursing & Feeding	✓	❹	Staff knowledge
Safety & Babycare	✓	❹	Customer service
Clothing, Shoes & Accessories	✓	❸	Decor
Books, Toys & Entertainment	✓		

WWW.CHILDRENSORCHARD.COM

BRUNSWICK—3654 CENTER RD (OFF RT 71); 330.273.2288; M 10-6, T 10-8, W 10-6, TH 10-8, F-SA 10-6, SU 1-5; PARKING LOT

Costco ★★★½☆

"...dependable place for bulk diapers, wipes and formula at discount prices... clothing selection is very hit-or-miss... avoid shopping there during nights and weekends if possible, because parking and checkout lines are brutal... they don't have a huge selection of brands, but the brands they do have are almost always in stock and at a great price... lowest prices around for diapers and formula... kid's clothing tends to be picked through, but it's worth looking for great deals on name-brand items like Carter's..."

Furniture, Bedding & Decor	✓	$$	Prices
Gear & Equipment	✓	❸	Product availability
Nursing & Feeding	✓	❸	Staff knowledge
Safety & Babycare	✓	❸	Customer service
Clothing, Shoes & Accessories	✓	❷	Decor
Books, Toys & Entertainment	✓		

WWW.COSTCO.COM

AVON—35804 DETROIT RD (AT CENTER RD); 440.930.0103; M-F 10-8:30, SA 9:30-6, SU 10-6

Dandy Lion Clothing & Gift Company ★★★★★

"...cute little shop in downtown Medina... upscale baby and maternity fashions... LeTop, Sweet Potatoes, Cachcach... cool gift selection... I generally find a couple extra items to stock up for baby showers... well organized..."

Furniture, Bedding & Decor	✓	$$$$	Prices
Gear & Equipment	✓	❸	Product availability
Nursing & Feeding	✗	❸	Staff knowledge
Safety & Babycare	✗	❸	Customer service
Clothing, Shoes & Accessories	✓	❺	Decor
Books, Toys & Entertainment	✓		

MEDINA—233 S COURT ST (AT W WASHINGTON ST); 330.723.3335; M-SA 10-5 ; STREET PARKING & LOT SOUTH OF STORE

Dillard's

❝...this store has beautiful clothes, and if you catch a sale, you can get great quality clothes at super bargain prices... good customer service and helpful staff... a huge selection of merchandise for boys and girls... nice layette department... some furnishings like little tables and chairs... beautiful displays... the best part is that in addition to shopping for your kids, you can also shop for yourself... ❞

Furniture, Bedding & Decor	✓	$$$	Prices
Gear & Equipment	✗	❹	Product availability
Nursing & Feeding	✗	❸	Staff knowledge
Safety & Babycare	✗	❹	Customer service
Clothing, Shoes & Accessories	✓	❹	Decor
Books, Toys & Entertainment	✓		

WWW.DILLARDS.COM

ELYRIA—4000 MIDWAY MALL (AT MIDWAY BLVD); 440.324.5711; M-SA 10-9, SU 12-6

Ginger Bread House

❝...great spot for resale clothes... any items that I have had there on consignment have sold very quickly and at a good price... ❞

Furniture, Bedding & Decor	✓	$	Prices
Gear & Equipment	✓	❸	Product availability
Nursing & Feeding	✓	❹	Staff knowledge
Safety & Babycare	✓	❸	Customer service
Clothing, Shoes & Accessories	✓	❹	Decor
Books, Toys & Entertainment	✓		

MEDINA—309 S BROADWAY ST (AT SMITH RD); 330.725.4622; M-SA 10-4

JCPenney

❝...always a good place to find clothes and other baby basics... the registry process was seamless... staff is generally friendly but the lines always seem long and slow... they don't have the greatest selection of toddler clothes, but their baby section is great... we had some damaged furniture delivered but customer service was easy and accommodating... a pretty limited selection of gear, but what they have is priced right... ❞

Furniture, Bedding & Decor	✓	$$	Prices
Gear & Equipment	✓	❸	Product availability
Nursing & Feeding	✓	❸	Staff knowledge
Safety & Babycare	✓	❸	Customer service
Clothing, Shoes & Accessories	✓	❸	Decor
Books, Toys & Entertainment	✓		

WWW.JCPENNEY.COM

ELYRIA—4500 MIDWAY MALL (AT MIDWAY MALL); 440.324.5736; M-SA 10-9, SU 11:30-5:30; PARKING LOT

Kohl's

❝...nice one-stop shopping for the whole family—everything from clothing to baby gear... great sales on clothing and a good selection of higher-end brands... stylish, inexpensive clothes for babies through 24 months... very easy shopping experience... dirt-cheap sales and

participate in our survey at

clearance prices... nothing super fancy, but just right for those everyday romper outfits... Graco, Eddie Bauer and other well-known brands... "

Furniture, Bedding & Decor	✓	$$	Prices
Gear & Equipment	✓	❹	Product availability
Nursing & Feeding	✓	❸	Staff knowledge
Safety & Babycare	✓	❸	Customer service
Clothing, Shoes & Accessories	✓	❸	Decor
Books, Toys & Entertainment	✓		

WWW.KOHLS.COM

AVON—35906 DETROIT RD (AT CENTER RD); 440.937.4166; M-SA 8-10, SU 10-8; FREE PARKING

MEDINA—4095 PEARL RD (AT FENN RD); 330.722.1977; M-SA 8-10, SU 10-8; FREE PARKING

Old Navy

" _...hip and 'in' clothes for infants and tots... plenty of steals on clearance items... T-shirts and pants for $10 or less... busy, busy, busy—long lines, especially on weekends... nothing fancy and you won't mind when your kids get down and dirty in these clothes... easy to wash, decent quality... you can shop for your baby, your toddler, your teen and yourself all at the same time... clothes are especially affordable when you hit their sales (post-holiday sales are amazing!)..._ "

Furniture, Bedding & Decor	✗	$$	Prices
Gear & Equipment	✗	❹	Product availability
Nursing & Feeding	✗	❸	Staff knowledge
Safety & Babycare	✗	❸	Customer service
Clothing, Shoes & Accessories	✗	❸	Decor
Books, Toys & Entertainment	✓		

WWW.OLDNAVY.COM

AVON—35852 DETROIT RD (OFF MIDDLETON DR); 440.937.0223; M-SA 10-9, SU 11-6

MEDINA—1155 N COURT ST (AT ROUTE 42); 330.723.0470; PARKING LOT

Playground World ★★★★★

" _...if you are looking for a playhouse or jungle gym, this is a good place to start... they also have lots of other toys from stuffed animals to trains... Brio and Gund... everything from kitchens to riding toys, fun for toddler and up... lots of plastic... fair prices..._ "

Furniture, Bedding & Decor	✗	$$$$	Prices
Gear & Equipment	✗	❹	Product availability
Nursing & Feeding	✗	❹	Staff knowledge
Safety & Babycare	✗	❹	Customer service
Clothing, Shoes & Accessories	✗	❹	Decor
Books, Toys & Entertainment	✓		

WWW.PGWORLD.COM

AVON—1014 JAYCOX RD (AT AVON COMMERCE PKWY); 440.937.5760; M-T 10-6, TH-F 10-6, SA 10-4, SU 11-4; PARKING LOT

MEDINA—2570 MEDINA RD (AT WINDFALL RD); 330.725.3388; M-T 10-5, TH-F 10-5, SA 10-4; PARKING LOT

Sears

" _...a decent selection of clothes and basic baby equipment... check out the Kids Club program—it's a great way to save money... you go to Sears to save money, not to be pampered... the quality of their merchandise is better than Wal-Mart, but don't expect anything too special or different... not much in terms of gear, but tons of well-priced baby and toddler clothing..._ "

Furniture, Bedding & Decor	✓	$$	Prices
Gear & Equipment	✓	❸	Product availability

Nursing & Feeding .... ✓ ❸ .... Staff knowledge
Safety & Babycare .... ✓ ❸ ....Customer service
Clothing, Shoes & Accessories ...... ✓ ❸ .... Decor
Books, Toys & Entertainment .... ✓
WWW.SEARS.COM

ELYRIA—4900 MIDWAY MALL (AT MIDWAY MALL); 440.324.1600; M-F 10-9,
SA 10-6, SU 11-5

Target

"...*our favorite place to shop for kids' stuff—good selection and very
affordable... guilt-free shopping—kids grow so fast so I don't want to
pay high department-store prices... everything from diapers and sippy
cups to car seats and strollers... easy return policy... generally helpful
staff, but you don't go for the service—you go for the prices... decent
registry that won't freak your friends out with outrageous prices... easy,
convenient shopping for well-priced items... all the big-box brands
available—Graco, Evenflo, Eddie Bauer, etc....* **"**

Furniture, Bedding & Decor .... ✓ $$.. Prices
Gear & Equipment .... ✓ ❹ ....Product availability
Nursing & Feeding .... ✓ ❸ .... Staff knowledge
Safety & Babycare .... ✓ ❸ ....Customer service
Clothing, Shoes & Accessories ...... ✓ ❸ .... Decor
Books, Toys & Entertainment .... ✓
WWW.TARGET.COM

AVON—35830 DETROIT RD (AT AVON COMMONS); 440.937.4301; M-SA 8-10,
SU 8-9; PARKING LOT

ELYRIA—240 MARKET DR (AT W RIVER RD); 440.324.1000; M-SA 8-10, SU 8-
9; PARKING LOT

MEDINA—1015 N COURT ST (AT REAGAN PKWY); 330.722.7539; M-SA 8-10,
SU 8-9; PARKING LOT

Portage & Summit

★★★★★

"lila picks"

- ★ Babies R Us
- ★ Baby Tyme Furniture
- ★ My Little Red Wagon
- ★ USA Baby

B J Wholesale Club ★★★★☆

"...*best place in town for diapers, wipes and formula... books, toys, car seats and cute clothes galore... affordable prices... this is a 'wholesale club' so you have to join ($40/year) or pay an extra 15 percent surcharge for a single day of shopping... what it lacks in service, it makes up for in savings...* **"**

Furniture, Bedding & Decor	✓	$ .... Prices
Gear & Equipment	✓	❺ .... Product availability
Nursing & Feeding	✓	❸ .... Staff knowledge
Safety & Babycare	✓	❹ .... Customer service
Clothing, Shoes & Accessories	✓	❸ .... Decor
Books, Toys & Entertainment	✓		

WWW.BJS.COM

AKRON—1677 HOME AVE (AT SUCCESS RD); 330.926.6000; M-SA 8-10, SU 8-9; PARKING LOT

Babies R Us ★★★★★

"...*everything baby under one roof... they have a wide selection and carry most 'mainstream' items such as Graco, Fisher-Price, Avent and Britax... great customer service—given how big the stores are, I was pleasantly surprised at how attentive the staff was... easy return policy... super busy on weekends so try to visit on a weekday for the best service... keep an eye out for great coupons, deals and frequent sales... easy and comprehensive registry... shopping here is so easy—you've got to check it out...* **"**

Furniture, Bedding & Decor	✓	$$$ .... Prices
Gear & Equipment	✓	❹ .... Product availability
Nursing & Feeding	✓	❹ .... Staff knowledge
Safety & Babycare	✓	❹ .... Customer service
Clothing, Shoes & Accessories	✓	❹ .... Decor
Books, Toys & Entertainment	✓		

WWW.BABIESRUS.COM

AURORA—7055 MARKET PL DR (AT THE 4 CORNERS PLZ); 330.995.4725; M-SA 9:30-9:30, SU 11-7; PARKING LOT

Baby Depot At Burlington Coat Factory

"...a large, 'super store' layout with a ton of baby gear... wide aisles, packed shelves, barely existent customer service and awesome prices... everything from bottles, car seats and strollers to gliders, cribs and clothes... I always find something worth getting... a little disorganized and hard to locate items you're looking for... the staff is not always knowledgeable about their merchandise... return policy is store credit only... **"**

Furniture, Bedding & Decor	✓	$$ .... Prices
Gear & Equipment	✓	❸ .... Product availability
Nursing & Feeding	✓	❸ .... Staff knowledge
Safety & Babycare	✓	❸ .... Customer service
Clothing, Shoes & Accessories	✓	❸ .... Decor
Books, Toys & Entertainment	✓	

WWW.BABYDEPOT.COM

CUYAHOGA FALLS—510 HOWE AVE (AT TALLMADGE RD); 330.920.4213; M-SA 10-9:30, SU 11-6; FREE PARKING

Baby Tyme Furniture

"...cribs, rockers, bedding and furniture galore... knowledgeable staff and uncompromised customer service... family-owned and operated and it shows—their customer service is great... a nice simple shop with a great selection of furnishings... **"**

Furniture, Bedding & Decor	✓	$$$ .... Prices
Gear & Equipment	✗	❺ .... Product availability
Nursing & Feeding	✗	❺ .... Staff knowledge
Safety & Babycare	✗	❺ .... Customer service
Clothing, Shoes & Accessories	✗	❺ .... Decor
Books, Toys & Entertainment	✗	

WWW.BABYTYMEFURNITURE.COM

HARTVILLE—878 W MAPLE ST (AT KENT AVE); 330.877.0330; M-F 10-8, SA 10-6, SU 12-5

BabyGap/GapKids

"...colorful baby and toddler clothing in clean, well-lit stores... great return policy... it's the Gap, so you know what you're getting—colorful, cute and well-made clothing... best place for baby hats... prices are reasonable especially since there's always a sale of some sort going on... sales, sales, sales—frequent and fantastic... everything I'm looking for in infant clothing—snap crotches, snaps up the front, all natural fabrics and great styling... fun seasonal selections—a great place to shop for gifts as well as for your own kids... although it can get busy, staff generally seem accommodating and helpful... **"**

Furniture, Bedding & Decor	✗	$$$ .... Prices
Gear & Equipment	✗	❹ .... Product availability
Nursing & Feeding	✗	❹ .... Staff knowledge
Safety & Babycare	✗	❹ .... Customer service
Clothing, Shoes & Accessories	✓	❹ .... Decor
Books, Toys & Entertainment	✗	

WWW.GAP.COM

AKRON—2000 BRITTAIN RD (NEAR HOWE RD); 330.633.8656; FREE PARKING

FAIRLAWN—3265 W MARKET ST (AT SUMMIT MALL); 330.864.9047; FREE PARKING

Carter's

"...always a great selection of inexpensive baby basics—everything from clothing to linens... I always find something at 'giveaway prices'

during one of their frequent sales... busy and crowded—it can be a chaotic shopping experience... 30 to 50 percent less than what you would pay at other boutiques... I bought five pieces of baby clothing for less than $40... durable, adorable and affordable... most stores have a small play area for kids in center of store so you can get your shopping done... **"**

Furniture, Bedding & Decor	✓	$$	Prices
Gear & Equipment	✗	❹	Product availability
Nursing & Feeding	✗	❹	Staff knowledge
Safety & Babycare	✗	❹	Customer service
Clothing, Shoes & Accessories	✓	❹	Decor
Books, Toys & Entertainment	✓		

WWW.CARTERS.COM

AURORA—549 S CHILLICOTHE RD (BTWN KINGSTON & AURORA HUDSON); 330.562.9036; FREE PARKING

Children's Orchard ★★★½☆

"...*a friendly resale boutique... the clothes and gear are super clean and sold at amazing prices... amazing prices on clothing that is hardly used and practically brand new... shoes, toys, furniture, hair pretties, crib sets, etc... fantastic deals on well-selected used items... prices are great and you can pretty much always find something useful... a great place to buy those everyday play outfits... a lot of name brands at steeply discounted prices...* **"**

Furniture, Bedding & Decor	✓	$$	Prices
Gear & Equipment	✓	❸	Product availability
Nursing & Feeding	✓	❹	Staff knowledge
Safety & Babycare	✓	❹	Customer service
Clothing, Shoes & Accessories	✓	❸	Decor
Books, Toys & Entertainment	✓		

WWW.CHILDRENSORCHARD.COM

HUDSON—118 W STSBORO ST (AT HUDSON VALLEY SHOPPING CTR); 330.656.5170; FREE PARKING

Children's Place, The ★★★½☆

"...*great bargains on cute clothing... shoes, socks, swimsuits, sunglasses and everything in between... lots of '3 for $20' type deals on sleepers, pants and mix-and-match separates... so much more affordable than the other 'big chains'... don't expect the most unique stuff here, but it wears and washes well... cheap clothing for cheap prices... you can leave the store with bags full of clothes without putting a huge dent in your wallet...* **"**

Furniture, Bedding & Decor	✗	$$	Prices
Gear & Equipment	✗	❹	Product availability
Nursing & Feeding	✗	❹	Staff knowledge
Safety & Babycare	✗	❹	Customer service
Clothing, Shoes & Accessories	✓	❹	Decor
Books, Toys & Entertainment	✓		

WWW.CHILDRENSPLACE.COM

AKRON—2000 BRITTAIN RD (OFF HOWE AVE); 330.633.1753; FREE PARKING

AURORA—549 S CHILLICOTHE RD (NEAR HARMON MIDDLE SCHOOL); 330.562.2796; FREE PARKING

FAIRLAWN—3265 W MARKET ST (AT SUMMIT MALL); 330.864.0440; FREE PARKING

Dillard's ★★★★☆

"...*this store has beautiful clothes, and if you catch a sale, you can get great quality clothes at super bargain prices... good customer service and helpful staff... a huge selection of merchandise for boys and girls... nice layette department... some furnishings like little tables and chairs...*

beautiful displays... the best part is that in addition to shopping for your kids, you can also shop for yourself... **"**

Furniture, Bedding & Decor	✓	$$$	Prices
Gear & Equipment	✗	❹	Product availability
Nursing & Feeding	✗	❸	Staff knowledge
Safety & Babycare	✗	❹	Customer service
Clothing, Shoes & Accessories	✓	❹	Decor
Books, Toys & Entertainment	✓		

WWW.DILLARDS.COM

AKRON—2400 ROMIG RD (AT ROLLING ACRES MALL); 330.745.1360; M-SA 11-7, SU 12-6

AKRON—3265 W MARKET ST (AT SUMMIT MALL); 330.867.3300; M-SA 10-9, SU 12-6

Gymboree

"*...beautiful clothing and great quality... colorful and stylish baby and kids wear... lots of fun birthday gift ideas... easy exchange and return policy... items usually go on sale pretty quickly... save money with Gymbucks... many stores have a play area which makes shopping with my kids fun (let alone feasible)...* **"**

Furniture, Bedding & Decor	✗	$$$	Prices
Gear & Equipment	✗	❹	Product availability
Nursing & Feeding	✗	❹	Staff knowledge
Safety & Babycare	✗	❹	Customer service
Clothing, Shoes & Accessories	✓	❹	Decor
Books, Toys & Entertainment	✓		

WWW.GYMBOREE.COM

FAIRLAWN—3265 W MARKET ST (AT SUMMIT MALL); 330.869.6440; FREE PARKING

JCPenney

"*...always a good place to find clothes and other baby basics... the registry process was seamless... staff is generally friendly but the lines always seem long and slow... they don't have the greatest selection of toddler clothes, but their baby section is great... we had some damaged furniture delivered but customer service was easy and accommodating... a pretty limited selection of gear, but what they have is priced right...* **"**

Furniture, Bedding & Decor	✓	$$	Prices
Gear & Equipment	✓	❸	Product availability
Nursing & Feeding	✓	❸	Staff knowledge
Safety & Babycare	✓	❸	Customer service
Clothing, Shoes & Accessories	✓	❸	Decor
Books, Toys & Entertainment	✓		

WWW.JCPENNEY.COM

AKRON—1500 CANTON RD (OFF WATERLOO RD); 330.733.6227; M-SA 10-9, SU 12-5

AKRON—2000 BRITTAIN RD (AT CHAPEL HILL MALL); 330.633.7700; M-SA 10-9, SU 12-6

Kohl's

"*...nice one-stop shopping for the whole family—everything from clothing to baby gear... great sales on clothing and a good selection of higher-end brands... stylish, inexpensive clothes for babies through 24 months... very easy shopping experience... dirt-cheap sales and clearance prices... nothing super fancy, but just right for those everyday romper outfits... Graco, Eddie Bauer and other well-known brands...* **"**

Furniture, Bedding & Decor	✓	$$	Prices
Gear & Equipment	✓	❹	Product availability
Nursing & Feeding	✓	❸	Staff knowledge

participate in our survey at

Safety & Babycare	✓	❸	Customer service
Clothing, Shoes & Accessories	✓	❸	Decor
Books, Toys & Entertainment	✓		

WWW.KOHLS.COM

AURORA—7005 N AURORA RD (OFF PETTIBONE RD); 330.562.4055; M-SA 8-10, SU 10-8; FREE PARKING

STOW—4240 KENT RD (AT STOW-KENT SHOPPING CTR); 330.688.0386; M-SA 8-10, SU 10-8; FREE PARKING

My Little Red Wagon ★★★★★

"...a cool toy store with less common items... lots of wood and learning toys... everything from Thomas trains to games and wooden doll houses... if you're looking for a birthday party gift then this definitely is the place to check out... the salespeople always have good suggestions... **"**

Furniture, Bedding & Decor	✗	$$$	Prices
Gear & Equipment	✗	❸	Product availability
Nursing & Feeding	✗	❸	Staff knowledge
Safety & Babycare	✗	❸	Customer service
Clothing, Shoes & Accessories	✗	❸	Decor
Books, Toys & Entertainment	✓		

WWW.MYLITTLEREDWAGON.COM

STOW—4317 KENT RD (AT FISHCREEK RD); 330.688.5506; M-TH 10-8, F-SA 10-9, SU 12-5

Old Navy ★★★★☆

"...hip and 'in' clothes for infants and tots... plenty of steals on clearance items... T-shirts and pants for $10 or less... busy, busy, busy—long lines, especially on weekends... nothing fancy and you won't mind when your kids get down and dirty in these clothes... easy to wash, decent quality... you can shop for your baby, your toddler, your teen and yourself all at the same time... clothes are especially affordable when you hit their sales (post-holiday sales are amazing!)... **"**

Furniture, Bedding & Decor	✗	$$	Prices
Gear & Equipment	✗	❹	Product availability
Nursing & Feeding	✗	❸	Staff knowledge
Safety & Babycare	✗	❸	Customer service
Clothing, Shoes & Accessories	✓	❸	Decor
Books, Toys & Entertainment	✗		

WWW.OLDNAVY.COM

AKRON—2000 BRITTIAN RD (AT CHAPEL HILL MALL); 330.630.5301; M-SA 9-9, SU 10-6

AKRON—3881 MEDINA RD (AT BROOKMONT RD); 330.666.3899; M-SA 9-9, SU 10-6

Once Upon A Child ★★★★☆

"...new and used items... the place for bargain baby items in like-new condition... a great bargain spot with a wide variety of clothes for baby... some inexpensive furniture... good selection, staff and prices... cluttered and hard to get through the store with kids... good toys and gear... some items are definitely more than 'gently used'... a kid's play area... good end-of-season sales... expect to sort through items... cash for your old items... **"**

Furniture, Bedding & Decor	✓	$$	Prices
Gear & Equipment	✓	❸	Product availability
Nursing & Feeding	✗	❹	Staff knowledge
Safety & Babycare	✗	❹	Customer service
Clothing, Shoes & Accessories	✓	❸	Decor
Books, Toys & Entertainment	✓		

STOW—4272 KENT RD (AT STOW-KENT SHOPPING CTR); 330.688.7176; M-F 10-8, SA 10-6, SU 12-5

Oshkosh B'gosh

"...cute, sturdy clothes for infants and toddlers... frequent sales make their high-quality merchandise a lot more affordable... doesn't every American kid have to get a pair of their overalls?.. great selection of cute clothes for boys... you can't go wrong here—their clothing is fun and worth the price... customer service is pretty hit-or-miss from store to store... we always walk out of here with something fun and colorful... **"**

Furniture, Bedding & Decor	✗	$$$	Prices
Gear & Equipment	✗	❹	Product availability
Nursing & Feeding	✗	❹	Staff knowledge
Safety & Babycare	✗	❹	Customer service
Clothing, Shoes & Accessories	✓	❹	Decor
Books, Toys & Entertainment	✗		

WWW.OSHKOSHBGOSH.COM

AURORA—549 S CHILLICOTHE RD (BTWN KINGSTON & AURORA HUDSON RD); 330.562.8018; M-SA 10-9, SU 11-6

Sears

"...a decent selection of clothes and basic baby equipment... check out the Kids Club program—it's a great way to save money... you go to Sears to save money, not to be pampered... the quality of their merchandise is better than Wal-Mart, but don't expect anything too special or different... not much in terms of gear, but tons of well-priced baby and toddler clothing... **"**

Furniture, Bedding & Decor	✓	$$	Prices
Gear & Equipment	✓	❸	Product availability
Nursing & Feeding	✓	❸	Staff knowledge
Safety & Babycare	✓	❸	Customer service
Clothing, Shoes & Accessories	✓	❸	Decor
Books, Toys & Entertainment	✓		

WWW.SEARS.COM

AKRON—2000 BRITTAIN RD (AT CHAPEL HILL MALL); 330.630.4700; M-SA 10-9, SU 11-6

Stride Rite Shoes

"...wonderful selection of baby and toddler shoes... sandals, sneakers, and even special-occasion shoes... decent quality shoes that last... they know a lot about kids' shoes and take the time to get it right—they always measure my son's feet before fittings... store sizes vary, but they always have something in stock that works... they've even special ordered shoes for my daughter... a fun 'first shoe' buying experience... **"**

Furniture, Bedding & Decor	✗	$$$	Prices
Gear & Equipment	✗	❹	Product availability
Nursing & Feeding	✗	❹	Staff knowledge
Safety & Babycare	✗	❹	Customer service
Clothing, Shoes & Accessories	✓	❹	Decor
Books, Toys & Entertainment	✗		

WWW.STRIDERITE.COM

AKRON—2000 BRITTAIN RD (AT CHAPEL HILL MALL); 330.633.7171; M-SA 10-9, SU 12-6

MOGADORE—2131 PALM RD (AT RANDOLPH RD); 440.528.0023; M-F 10-7, SA 10-6, SU 12-5

Target ★★★★☆

"...our favorite place to shop for kids' stuff—good selection and very affordable... guilt-free shopping—kids grow so fast so I don't want to pay high department-store prices... everything from diapers and sippy cups to car seats and strollers... easy return policy... generally helpful staff, but you don't go for the service—you go for the prices... decent registry that won't freak your friends out with outrageous prices... easy, convenient shopping for well-priced items... all the big-box brands available—Graco, Evenflo, Eddie Bauer, etc....**"**

Furniture, Bedding & Decor	✓	$$	Prices
Gear & Equipment	✓	❹	Product availability
Nursing & Feeding	✓	❸	Staff knowledge
Safety & Babycare	✓	❸	Customer service
Clothing, Shoes & Accessories	✓	❸	Decor
Books, Toys & Entertainment	✓		

WWW.TARGET.COM

AKRON—2400 ROMIG RD (AT ROLLING ACRES MALL); 330.745.0495; M-SA 8-10, SU 8-9

CUYAHOGA FALLS—449 HOWE AVE (OFF RT 8); 330.928.0014; M-SA 8-10, SU 8-9

FAIRLAWN—2801 W MARKET ST (AT MILLER RD); 330.865.9001; M-SA 8-10, SU 8-9

STOW—4200 KENT RD (AT STOW-KENT SHOPPING CTR); 330.688.5928; M-SA 8-10, SU 8-9

Three Elysabethe's Baby And Kids Shop ★★★★☆

"...splurge on a unique gift at this cute baby shop... close to the Aurora Farms outlet, but far from outlet prices!.. adorable stationery for baby announcements... a great escape from the 'standard' baby accessories at the chains... staff is helpful...**"**

Furniture, Bedding & Decor	✓	$$$$	Prices
Gear & Equipment	✗	❸	Product availability
Nursing & Feeding	✗	❺	Staff knowledge
Safety & Babycare	✗	❺	Customer service
Clothing, Shoes & Accessories	✗	❺	Decor
Books, Toys & Entertainment	✓		

AURORA—196 S CHILLICOTHE RD (AT RT 306); 330.995.0547; M-SA 10-6, SU 12-5; PARKING LOT

USA Baby ★★★★★

"...they carry an extensive selection of high-end nursery products such as furniture, bedding, accessories and highchairs... popular place to do all the shopping for your nursery... the staff knows their products well and can help you sort through their vast selection... allow plenty of time for your products to arrive, especially the big-ticket items (they offer loaners while you wait for your order to arrive)... they have great sales a few times a year and will match competitor prices... good selection, especially if you're getting ready to set up your nursery...**"**

Furniture, Bedding & Decor	✓	$$$$	Prices
Gear & Equipment	✓	❹	Product availability
Nursing & Feeding	✓	❹	Staff knowledge
Safety & Babycare	✓	❹	Customer service
Clothing, Shoes & Accessories	✗	❹	Decor
Books, Toys & Entertainment	✓		

WWW.USABABY.COM

CUYAHOGA FALLS—2929 STATE RD (AT GRAHAM RD); 330.928.2229; M-T TH 10-8, W F-SA 10-6, SU 12-4; FREE PARKING

Online

★ ★ ★ ★ ★

"lila picks"

★ babycenter.com ★ babystyle.com
★ babyuniverse.com ★ joggingstroller.com

ababy.com

Furniture, Bedding & Decor .... ✓	✓ .... Gear & Equipment
Nursing & Feeding .... ✗	✓ .... Safety & Babycare
Clothing, Shoes & Accessories ...... ✓	✗ .... Books, Toys & Entertainment

aikobaby.com ★★★☆☆

"...high end clothes that are so cute...everything from Catamini to Jack and Lily... you can find super expensive infant and baby clothes at discounted prices... amazing selection of diaper bags so you don't have to look like a frumpy mom (or dad)... **"**

Furniture, Bedding & Decor .... ✗	✓ .... Gear & Equipment
Nursing & Feeding .... ✗	✗ .... Safety & Babycare
Clothing, Shoes & Accessories ...... ✓	✗ .... Books, Toys & Entertainment

albeebaby.com ★★★★☆

"...they offer a really comprehensive selection of baby gear... their prices are some of the best online... great discounts on Maclarens before the new models come out... good product availability—fast shipping and easy transactions... the site is pretty easy to use... the prices are surprisingly great... **"**

Furniture, Bedding & Decor .... ✓	✓ .... Gear & Equipment
Nursing & Feeding .... ✓	✓ .... Safety & Babycare
Clothing, Shoes & Accessories ...... ✓	✓ .... Books, Toys & Entertainment

amazon.com ★★★★½

"...unless you've been living under a rock, you know that in addition to books, Amazon carries an amazing amount of baby stuff too... they have the best prices and offer free shipping on bigger purchases... you can even buy used items for dirt cheap... I always read the comments written by others—they're very useful in helping make my decisions... I love Amazon for just about everything, but their baby selection only carries the big box standards... **"**

Furniture, Bedding & Decor .... ✗	✓ .... Gear & Equipment
Nursing & Feeding .... ✓	✓ .... Safety & Babycare
Clothing, Shoes & Accessories ...... ✓	✓ .... Books, Toys & Entertainment

arunningstroller.com ★★★★½

"...the prices are very competitive and the customer service is great... I talked to them on the phone for a while and they totally hooked me up with the right model... if you're looking for a new stroller, look no further... talk to Marilyn—she's the best... shipping costs are reasonable and their prices overall are good... **"**

Furniture, Bedding & Decor .... ✓   ✓ .... Gear & Equipment
Nursing & Feeding .... ✗   ✗ .... Safety & Babycare
Clothing, Shoes & Accessories....... ✗   ✗ .... Books, Toys & Entertainment

babiesinthesun.com ★★★★☆

"...one-stop shopping for cloth diapers... run by a fantastic woman who had 3 cloth diapered babies herself and is a wealth of knowledge... if you live in South Florida, the owner will let you into her home to see the merchandise and ask questions... great selection and the customer service is the best... **"**

Furniture, Bedding & Decor .... ✗   ✓ .... Gear & Equipment
Nursing & Feeding .... ✗   ✓ .... Safety & Babycare
Clothing, Shoes & Accessories....... ✗   ✗ .... Books, Toys & Entertainment

babiesrus.com ★★★★☆

"...terrific web site with all the baby gear you'll need... registering online made it easy for my family and friends... getting the registry activated was a bit tricky... super convenient and ideal for the moms-to-be who are on bedrest... web site prices are comparable to in-store prices... shipping is usually free... a very efficient way to buy and send baby gifts... our local Babies R Us said they will accept returns if they carry the same item... not all online items are available in your local store... **"**

Furniture, Bedding & Decor .... ✓   ✓ .... Gear & Equipment
Nursing & Feeding .... ✓   ✓ .... Safety & Babycare
Clothing, Shoes & Accessories....... ✓   ✓ .... Books, Toys & Entertainment

babiestravellite.com ★★★★½

"...caters to traveling families... they deliver baby items to your hotel room anywhere in the country... all of the different baby supplies you will need when you travel with a baby or a toddler... they sell almost every major brand for each product and their prices are sometimes cheaper than you would find at your local store... **"**

Furniture, Bedding & Decor .... ✗   ✗ .... Gear & Equipment
Nursing & Feeding .... ✓   ✓ .... Safety & Babycare
Clothing, Shoes & Accessories....... ✗   ✓ .... Books, Toys & Entertainment

babyage.com ★★★★☆

"...fast shipping and the best prices around... flat rate shipping is great after the baby has arrived and you don't have time to go to the store... very attentive customer service... clearance items are a great deal (regular items are very competitive too)... ordering and delivery were super smooth... I usually check this web site before I purchase any baby gear... sign up for their newsletter and they'll notify you when they are having a sale... **"**

Furniture, Bedding & Decor .... ✓   ✓ .... Gear & Equipment
Nursing & Feeding .... ✓   ✓ .... Safety & Babycare
Clothing, Shoes & Accessories....... ✓   ✓ .... Books, Toys & Entertainment

babyant.com ★★★★☆

"...wide variety of brands and products available through their site... super easy to navigate... fun, whimsical ideas... nice people and helpful... easy to return items and you can call them with questions... often has the best prices and low shipping costs... **"**

Furniture, Bedding & Decor .... ✓   ✓ .... Gear & Equipment
Nursing & Feeding .... ✓   ✓ .... Safety & Babycare
Clothing, Shoes & Accessories....... ✓   ✓ .... Books, Toys & Entertainment

babybazaar.com

"...high-end baby stuff available on an easy-to-use web site... lots of European styles... quick processing and shipping... mom's tips, educational toys, exclusive favorites Bugaboo and Stokke...**"**

Furniture, Bedding & Decor	✓	✓	Gear & Equipment
Nursing & Feeding	✓	✓	Safety & Babycare
Clothing, Shoes & Accessories	✓	✓	Books, Toys & Entertainment

babybestbuy.com

Furniture, Bedding & Decor	✓	✓	Gear & Equipment
Nursing & Feeding	✓	✓	Safety & Babycare
Clothing, Shoes & Accessories	✓	✓	Books, Toys & Entertainment

babycatalog.com ★★★★☆

"...great deals on many essentials... wide selection of rockers but fewer options in other categories... the web site could be more user-friendly... customer service and delivery was fast and efficient... check out their seasonal specials... the baby club is a great way to save additional money... sign up for their wonderful pregnancy/new baby email newsletter... check this web site before you buy anywhere else...**"**

Furniture, Bedding & Decor	✓	✓	Gear & Equipment
Nursing & Feeding	✓	✓	Safety & Babycare
Clothing, Shoes & Accessories	✓	✓	Books, Toys & Entertainment

babycenter.com ★★★★★

"...a terrific selection of all things baby, plus quick shipping... free shipping on big orders... makes shopping convenient for new parents... web site is very user friendly... they always email you about sale items and special offers... lots of useful information for parents... carries everything you may need... online registry is simple, easy and a great way to get what you need... includes helpful products ratings by parents... they've created a nice online community in addition to their online store...**"**

Furniture, Bedding & Decor	✓	✓	Gear & Equipment
Nursing & Feeding	✓	✓	Safety & Babycare
Clothing, Shoes & Accessories	✓	✓	Books, Toys & Entertainment

babydepot.com ★★★☆☆

"...carries everything you'll find in a big department store but at cheaper prices and with everything all in one place... be certain you know what you want because returns can be difficult... site could be more user-friendly... online selection can differ from instore selection... love the online registry...**"**

Furniture, Bedding & Decor	✓	✓	Gear & Equipment
Nursing & Feeding	✓	✓	Safety & Babycare
Clothing, Shoes & Accessories	✓	✓	Books, Toys & Entertainment

babygeared.com

Furniture, Bedding & Decor	✓	✓	Gear & Equipment
Nursing & Feeding	✓	✓	Safety & Babycare
Clothing, Shoes & Accessories	✓	✓	Books, Toys & Entertainment

babyphd.com

Furniture, Bedding & Decor	✓	✗	Gear & Equipment
Nursing & Feeding	✗	✗	Safety & Babycare
Clothing, Shoes & Accessories	✓	✓	Books, Toys & Entertainment

babystyle.com ★★★★★

"...their web site is just like their stores—terrific... an excellent source for everything a parent needs... fantastic maternity and baby clothes...

participate in our survey at

they always respond quickly by email... their site seems to have even more merchandise than their stores... I started shopping on their site after receiving a gift card—very easy and convenient... wonderful selection... **99**

Furniture, Bedding & Decor .... ✓   ✓ .... Gear & Equipment
Nursing & Feeding .... ✓   ✓ .... Safety & Babycare
Clothing, Shoes & Accessories .... ✓   ✓ .... Books, Toys & Entertainment

babysupermall.com

Furniture, Bedding & Decor .... ✓   ✓ .... Gear & Equipment
Nursing & Feeding .... ✓   ✓ .... Safety & Babycare
Clothing, Shoes & Accessories .... ✓   ✓ .... Books, Toys & Entertainment

babyuniverse.com ★★★★★

66 *...nice large selection of specialty and basic items... easy-to-use web site with decent prices... carries Carter's clothes and many other popular brands... great bedding selection - they're one of the few places with the Kidsline bedding I wanted... adorable backpacks for toddlers and preschoolers... check out the site for strollers and car seats... this was my first online shopping experience and they made it so easy, convenient and fast, I was hooked... fine customer service... flat rate (if not free) shipping takes the 'ouch' factor out of those big ticket purchases...* **99**

Furniture, Bedding & Decor .... ✓   ✓ .... Gear & Equipment
Nursing & Feeding .... ✓   ✓ .... Safety & Babycare
Clothing, Shoes & Accessories .... ✓   ✓ .... Books, Toys & Entertainment

barebabies.com

Furniture, Bedding & Decor .... ✓   ✓ .... Gear & Equipment
Nursing & Feeding .... ✓   ✓ .... Safety & Babycare
Clothing, Shoes & Accessories .... ✓   ✓ .... Books, Toys & Entertainment

birthandbaby.com ★★★★☆

66 *...incredible site for buying a nursing bra... there is more information about different manufacturers than you can imagine... I've even received a phone call from the owner after placing an order to clarify something... free shipping, so it's easy to buy multiple sizes and send back the ones that don't fit... their selection of nursing bras is better than any other place I've found... if you are a hard to fit size, this is the place to go...* **99**

Furniture, Bedding & Decor .... ✗   ✓ .... Gear & Equipment
Nursing & Feeding .... ✓   ✓ .... Safety & Babycare
Clothing, Shoes & Accessories .... ✗   ✓ .... Books, Toys & Entertainment

blueberrybabies.com

Furniture, Bedding & Decor .... ✓   ✓ .... Gear & Equipment
Nursing & Feeding .... ✓   ✓ .... Safety & Babycare
Clothing, Shoes & Accessories .... ✓   ✓ .... Books, Toys & Entertainment

buybuybaby.com ★★★★⯪

66 *...this is the web site for the popular New York-based baby retailer... you name it, they've got it... all the items in their store can also be found on their web site... prices are fair - especially since things get shipped right to your door... we had some items that were damaged and their online customer service took care of it without any problems...* **99**

Furniture, Bedding & Decor .... ✓   ✓ .... Gear & Equipment
Nursing & Feeding .... ✓   ✓ .... Safety & Babycare
Clothing, Shoes & Accessories .... ✓   ✓ .... Books, Toys & Entertainment

childcarriers.com

Furniture, Bedding & Decor .... ✗   ✓ .... Gear & Equipment

| Nursing & Feeding ....✗ | ✗ ....Safety & Babycare |
| Clothing, Shoes & Accessories ....✗ | ✗ ....Books, Toys & Entertainment |

clothdiaper.com

Furniture, Bedding & Decor...........✗	✓ ....Gear & Equipment
Nursing & Feeding ....✓	✓ ....Safety & Babycare
Clothing, Shoes & Accessories ....✗	✗ ....Books, Toys & Entertainment

cocoacrayon.com

Furniture, Bedding & Decor...........✓	✓ ....Gear & Equipment
Nursing & Feeding ....✓	✓ ....Safety & Babycare
Clothing, Shoes & Accessories ......✓	✓ ....Books, Toys & Entertainment

cvs.com ★★★★☆

"...super convenient web site for any 'drug store' items... items are delivered in a reasonable amount of time... decent selection of baby products... prices are competitive and ordering online definitely beats making the trip out to the drugstore... order a bunch of stuff at a time so shipping is free... I used them for my baby announcements and everyone loved them... super easy to refill prescriptions... it was a real relief to order all my formula, baby wipes and diapers online... **"**

Furniture, Bedding & Decor...........✗	✗ ....Gear & Equipment
Nursing & Feeding ....✓	✓ ....Safety & Babycare
Clothing, Shoes & Accessories ....✗	✗ ....Books, Toys & Entertainment

dreamtimebaby.com

Furniture, Bedding & Decor...........✓	✓ ....Gear & Equipment
Nursing & Feeding ....✓	✓ ....Safety & Babycare
Clothing, Shoes & Accessories ......✓	✓ ....Books, Toys & Entertainment

drugstore.com ★★★★☆

Furniture, Bedding & Decor...........✗	✗ ....Gear & Equipment
Nursing & Feeding ....✓	✓ ....Safety & Babycare
Clothing, Shoes & Accessories ....✗	✗ ....Books, Toys & Entertainment

ebay.com ★★★★☆

"...great way to save money on everything from maternity clothes to breast pumps... be careful with whom you do business... it's always worth checking out what's available... I picked up a brand new jogger for dirt cheap... great deals to be had if you have patience to browse and be willing to resell or exchange what you don't like... baby stuff is easily found and often reasonably priced... keep an eye on shipping costs when you're bidding... **"**

Furniture, Bedding & Decor...........✓	✓ ....Gear & Equipment
Nursing & Feeding ....✓	✓ ....Safety & Babycare
Clothing, Shoes & Accessories ......✓	✓ ....Books, Toys & Entertainment

egiggle.com ★★★★☆

"...nice selection—not overwhelming... don't expect the big box store brands here—they carry higher-end, specialty items that you won't find elsewhere... smooth shopping experience... nice site—convenient and easy to use... **"**

Furniture, Bedding & Decor...........✓	✓ ....Gear & Equipment
Nursing & Feeding ....✓	✓ ....Safety & Babycare
Clothing, Shoes & Accessories ......✓	✓ ....Books, Toys & Entertainment

gagagifts.com ★★★★☆

"...great online store that carries fun clothes and unique gifts and toys for kids and adults... unique and special gifts like designer diaper bags, Whoozit learning toys and handmade quilts... this site makes gift buying incredibly easy—I'm done in less than 5 minutes... prices are high but products are special... **"**

Furniture, Bedding & Decor .... ✓	✓ .... Gear & Equipment	
Nursing & Feeding .... ✓	✓ .... Safety & Babycare	
Clothing, Shoes & Accessories .... ✓	✓ .... Books, Toys & Entertainment	

gap.com ★★★★☆

"...I love the Gap's online store—all the cool things in their stores available via my computer... terrific selection of boys and girls clothes plus cute shoes... you can find awesome deals and return online purchases to Gap stores... their clothes are very durable... it's easy to purchase items online and delivery is prompt... a very practical and affordable way to shop... site makes it easy to quickly find what you need... sign up for the weekly newsletter and you'll find out about online sales... "

Furniture, Bedding & Decor .... ✓	✓ .... Gear & Equipment
Nursing & Feeding .... ✗	✗ .... Safety & Babycare
Clothing, Shoes & Accessories .... ✓	✓ .... Books, Toys & Entertainment

geniusbabies.com ★★★⯨☆

"...the best selection available of developmental toys and gifts... the only place to order real puppets from the Baby Einstein video series... cool place for unique baby shower and birthday gifts... their site navigation could use an upgrade... "

Furniture, Bedding & Decor .... ✗	✗ .... Gear & Equipment
Nursing & Feeding .... ✗	✗ .... Safety & Babycare
Clothing, Shoes & Accessories .... ✗	✓ .... Books, Toys & Entertainment

gymboree.com ★★★★☆

"...beautiful clothing and great quality... colorful and stylish baby and kids wear... lots of fun birthday gift ideas... easy exchange and return policy... items usually go on sale pretty quickly... save money with gymbucks... many stores have a play area which makes shopping with my kids fun (let alone feasible)... "

Furniture, Bedding & Decor .... ✗	✗ .... Gear & Equipment
Nursing & Feeding .... ✗	✗ .... Safety & Babycare
Clothing, Shoes & Accessories .... ✓	✓ .... Books, Toys & Entertainment

hannaandersson.com

Furniture, Bedding & Decor .... ✓	✗ .... Gear & Equipment
Nursing & Feeding .... ✓	✗ .... Safety & Babycare
Clothing, Shoes & Accessories .... ✓	✓ .... Books, Toys & Entertainment

jcpenney.com

Furniture, Bedding & Decor .... ✓	✗ .... Gear & Equipment
Nursing & Feeding .... ✗	✓ .... Safety & Babycare
Clothing, Shoes & Accessories .... ✓	✗ .... Books, Toys & Entertainment

joggingstroller.com ★★★★★

"...an excellent resource when you're choosing a jogging stroller... the entire site is devoted to joggers... very helpful information that's worth checking whether you plan to buy from them or not... the best online guide for researching jogging strollers... includes helpful comparisons and parent reviews on the top strollers... "

Furniture, Bedding & Decor .... ✗	✓ .... Gear & Equipment
Nursing & Feeding .... ✗	✗ .... Safety & Babycare
Clothing, Shoes & Accessories .... ✗	✗ .... Books, Toys & Entertainment

kidsurplus.com

Furniture, Bedding & Decor .... ✓	✗ .... Gear & Equipment
Nursing & Feeding .... ✓	✗ .... Safety & Babycare
Clothing, Shoes & Accessories .... ✓	✓ .... Books, Toys & Entertainment

landofnod.com ★★★★☆

"...cool site with adorable and unique furnishings... hip kid style art work... fabulous furniture and bedding... the catalog is amusing and nicely laid out... lots of sweet selections for both boys and girls... good customer service... fun but small selection of music, books, toys and more... a great way to get ideas for putting rooms together... **"**

Furniture, Bedding & Decor ✓	✗	Gear & Equipment
Nursing & Feeding ✗	✗	Safety & Babycare
Clothing, Shoes & Accessories ✗	✓	Books, Toys & Entertainment

landsend.com ★★★★☆

"...carries the best quality in children's wear—their stuff lasts forever... durable and adorable clothing, shoes and bedding... they offer a huge variety of casual clothing and awesome pajamas... not as inexpensive as other sites, but you can't beat the quality... the very best diaper bags... site is easy to navigate and has great finds for the entire family... love the flannel sheets, maternity clothes and shoes for mom... **"**

Furniture, Bedding & Decor ✓	✗	Gear & Equipment
Nursing & Feeding ✗	✗	Safety & Babycare
Clothing, Shoes & Accessories ✓	✗	Books, Toys & Entertainment

letsgostrolling.com

Furniture, Bedding & Decor ✓	✓	Gear & Equipment
Nursing & Feeding ✓	✗	Safety & Babycare
Clothing, Shoes & Accessories ✓	✓	Books, Toys & Entertainment

llbean.com ★★★★☆

"...high quality clothing for babies, toddlers and kids at reasonable prices... the clothes are extremely durable and stand up to wear and tear very well... a great site for winter clothing and gear shopping... wonderful selection for older kids, too... fewer options for infants... an awesome way to shop for clothing basics... you can't beat the diaper bags... **"**

Furniture, Bedding & Decor ✗	✗	Gear & Equipment
Nursing & Feeding ✗	✗	Safety & Babycare
Clothing, Shoes & Accessories ✓	✗	Books, Toys & Entertainment

modernseed.com ★★★★½

"...it was fun finding many unique items for my son's nursery... I wanted a contemporary theme and they had lots of wonderful items including crib linens, wall art and lighting... the place to find super cool baby and kid stuff and the best place for modern nursery decor... they also carry children and adult clothing and furniture and toys... not cheap but one of my favorite places... **"**

Furniture, Bedding & Decor ✓	✓	Gear & Equipment
Nursing & Feeding ✓	✓	Safety & Babycare
Clothing, Shoes & Accessories ✓	✓	Books, Toys & Entertainment

naturalbaby-catalog.com ★★★½☆

"...all natural products—clothes, toys, herbal medicines, bathing, etc... fine quality and a great alternative to the usual products... site is fairly easy to navigate and has a good selection... dealing with returns is pretty painless... love the catalogue and the products... excellent customer service... lots of organic clothing made with natural materials... high quality shoes in a range of prices... **"**

Furniture, Bedding & Decor ✓	✓	Gear & Equipment
Nursing & Feeding ✓	✓	Safety & Babycare
Clothing, Shoes & Accessories ✓	✓	Books, Toys & Entertainment

netkidswear.com

Furniture, Bedding & Decor .... ✓	✓ .... Gear & Equipment
Nursing & Feeding .... ✓	✓ .... Safety & Babycare
Clothing, Shoes & Accessories .... ✓	✓ .... Books, Toys & Entertainment

nordstrom.com ★★★★☆

"...just like their stores, the site carries a great selection of high-quality items... you can't go wrong with Nordstrom—even online... quick shipping and easy site navigation... a little pricey, but great quality items... I've purchased a bunch of baby stuff from their website and have never had a problem... a great shoe selection for all ages... **"**

Furniture, Bedding & Decor .... ✓	✓ .... Gear & Equipment
Nursing & Feeding .... ✗	✓ .... Safety & Babycare
Clothing, Shoes & Accessories .... ✓	✓ .... Books, Toys & Entertainment

oldnavy.com ★★★★☆

"...shopping online with Old Navy makes it easy to find incredible bargains... site was easy to use and my products arrived quickly... site carries items that aren't necessarily available in their stores... an inexpensive way to get trendy baby clothes... you can return items directly to any store... check out the sale page of this web site for deep discounts on current season clothing... I signed up for the email savings and get free shipping several times a year... **"**

Furniture, Bedding & Decor .... ✗	✗ .... Gear & Equipment
Nursing & Feeding .... ✗	✗ .... Safety & Babycare
Clothing, Shoes & Accessories .... ✓	✗ .... Books, Toys & Entertainment

oliebollen.com ★★★★★

"...perfect for the busy mom looking for a fun baby shower gift... this online-only store has all the best brands—Catamini and Tea Collection to name a couple... great for gifts and home stuff, too... lots of style... very easy to use... 30 days full refund, 60 days store credit... **"**

Furniture, Bedding & Decor .... ✓	✗ .... Gear & Equipment
Nursing & Feeding .... ✓	✗ .... Safety & Babycare
Clothing, Shoes & Accessories .... ✓	✓ .... Books, Toys & Entertainment

onestepahead.com ★★★★★

"...one stop shopping site with everything parents are looking for... huge variety of items to choose from... I bought everything from a crib to a nursery bottle... high quality items, many of which are developmental in nature... great line of safety equipment... easy to order and fast delivery but you will pay for shipping... web site has helpful reviews... great site for hard to find items... **"**

Furniture, Bedding & Decor .... ✓	✓ .... Gear & Equipment
Nursing & Feeding .... ✓	✓ .... Safety & Babycare
Clothing, Shoes & Accessories .... ✓	✓ .... Books, Toys & Entertainment

peapods.com

Furniture, Bedding & Decor .... ✓	✓ .... Gear & Equipment
Nursing & Feeding .... ✗	✓ .... Safety & Babycare
Clothing, Shoes & Accessories .... ✓	✓ .... Books, Toys & Entertainment

pokkadots.com

Furniture, Bedding & Decor .... ✓	✓ .... Gear & Equipment
Nursing & Feeding .... ✓	✗ .... Safety & Babycare
Clothing, Shoes & Accessories .... ✓	✓ .... Books, Toys & Entertainment

poshtots.com ★★★★☆

"...incredible selection of whimsical and out-of-the-ordinary nursery decor... beautiful, unique designer room sets in multiple styles... they do boys and girls bedrooms... great for the baby that has everything—

including parents with an unlimited cash account... you can get great ideas about decor just from browsing the site, even if you don't buy... 🗩

Furniture, Bedding & Decor	✓	✓	Gear & Equipment
Nursing & Feeding	✓	✗	Safety & Babycare
Clothing, Shoes & Accessories	✓	✓	Books, Toys & Entertainment

potterybarnkids.com ★★★★⯪

🗩*...beautiful high end furniture and bedding... they have a way with matching everything perfectly and I am always a sucker for that look... adorable merchandise of great quality... you will get what you pay for: high quality furniture at high prices... web site is easy to navigate... items like hooded towels and plush blankets make this place special... if I could afford it I would buy everything in the store...* 🗩

Furniture, Bedding & Decor	✓	✓	Gear & Equipment
Nursing & Feeding	✗	✗	Safety & Babycare
Clothing, Shoes & Accessories	✗	✓	Books, Toys & Entertainment

preemie.com

Furniture, Bedding & Decor	✗	✓	Gear & Equipment
Nursing & Feeding	✓	✓	Safety & Babycare
Clothing, Shoes & Accessories	✓	✓	Books, Toys & Entertainment

rei.com

Furniture, Bedding & Decor	✗	✓	Gear & Equipment
Nursing & Feeding	✗	✗	Safety & Babycare
Clothing, Shoes & Accessories	✓	✓	Books, Toys & Entertainment

royalnursery.com ★★★⯪☆

🗩*...this used to be a store in San Diego and now it is only online... if you need a silver rattle, luxury baby blanket or shower gift—this is the place... a beautiful site with elegant baby clothes, jewelry, and gifts...love the hand print kits—they are my current favorite gift... high end baby wear and gear... be sure to check out the sale items...* 🗩

Furniture, Bedding & Decor	✓	✗	Gear & Equipment
Nursing & Feeding	✗	✓	Safety & Babycare
Clothing, Shoes & Accessories	✓	✓	Books, Toys & Entertainment

showeryourbaby.com

Furniture, Bedding & Decor	✓	✓	Gear & Equipment
Nursing & Feeding	✓	✓	Safety & Babycare
Clothing, Shoes & Accessories	✓	✓	Books, Toys & Entertainment

snipsnsnails.com ★★★★⯪

🗩*...a great boys clothing store for infants to 14 years old... clothes for every occasion, from casual to special occasion... pajamas and swimsuits, too... pricey, but upscale and fun... items on the web site are not always in stock ...* 🗩

Furniture, Bedding & Decor	✓	✗	Gear & Equipment
Nursing & Feeding	✗	✗	Safety & Babycare
Clothing, Shoes & Accessories	✓	✗	Books, Toys & Entertainment

strollerdepot.com

Furniture, Bedding & Decor	✗	✓	Gear & Equipment
Nursing & Feeding	✗	✗	Safety & Babycare
Clothing, Shoes & Accessories	✗	✓	Books, Toys & Entertainment

strollers4less.com ★★★⯪☆

🗩*...some of the best prices on strollers... I love this site... we purchased our stroller online for a lot less than it costs locally... online ordering went smoothly—from ordering through receiving... wide*

participate in our survey at

selection and some incredible deals... shipping is relatively fast... free shipping if you spend $100, which isn't hard to do... **99**

Furniture, Bedding & Decor	✗	✓	Gear & Equipment
Nursing & Feeding	✗	✗	Safety & Babycare
Clothing, Shoes & Accessories	✗	✓	Books, Toys & Entertainment

target.com ★★★★☆

66*...our favorite place to shop for kids stuff—good selection and very affordable... guilt free shopping—kids grow so fast so I don't want to pay high department store prices... everything from diapers and sippy cups to car seats and strollers... easy return policy... generally helpful staff, but you don't go for the service—you go for the prices... decent registry that won't freak your friends out with outrageous prices... easy, convenient shopping for well-priced items... all the big box brands available—Graco, Evenflo, Eddie Bauer, etc....* **99**

Furniture, Bedding & Decor	✓	✓	Gear & Equipment
Nursing & Feeding	✓	✓	Safety & Babycare
Clothing, Shoes & Accessories	✓	✓	Books, Toys & Entertainment

teddylux.com

Furniture, Bedding & Decor	✗	✗	Gear & Equipment
Nursing & Feeding	✗	✗	Safety & Babycare
Clothing, Shoes & Accessories	✗	✓	Books, Toys & Entertainment

thebabyhammock.com ★★★★☆

66*...a family owned business selling parent-tested products from morning sickness relief products to baby carriers, natural skincare, gift sets and more... fast friendly service... natural products and waldorf influenced toys...* **99**

Furniture, Bedding & Decor	✓	✓	Gear & Equipment
Nursing & Feeding	✓	✓	Safety & Babycare
Clothing, Shoes & Accessories	✓	✗	Books, Toys & Entertainment

thebabyoutlet.com

Furniture, Bedding & Decor	✗	✓	Gear & Equipment
Nursing & Feeding	✓	✓	Safety & Babycare
Clothing, Shoes & Accessories	✗	✓	Books, Toys & Entertainment

tinyride.com

Furniture, Bedding & Decor	✗	✓	Gear & Equipment
Nursing & Feeding	✓	✗	Safety & Babycare
Clothing, Shoes & Accessories	✗	✗	Books, Toys & Entertainment

toadsandtulips.com

Furniture, Bedding & Decor	✗	✗	Gear & Equipment
Nursing & Feeding	✗	✗	Safety & Babycare
Clothing, Shoes & Accessories	✗	✗	Books, Toys & Entertainment

toysrus.com ★★★★☆

66*...makes shopping incredibly easy... well organized site with discount prices... makes registering for gifts super simple... even more products are online than in the actual stores... check out the outlet section and coupon codes for even more discounts... I did most of my Christmas shopping here, paid no shipping and had my gifts delivered in 3 days... web site includes helpful toy reviews... use this to send your wish lists to relatives...* **99**

Furniture, Bedding & Decor	✓	✓	Gear & Equipment
Nursing & Feeding	✓	✓	Safety & Babycare
Clothing, Shoes & Accessories	✓	✓	Books, Toys & Entertainment

tuttibella.com

"...well designed web site with beautiful, original clothing, toys, bedding and accessories... cute vintage stuff for babies and kids... stylish designer goods from here and abroad... your child will stand out among the Baby Gap-clothed masses... gorgeous fabrics... a great place to find that perfect gift for someone special and stylish..."

Furniture, Bedding & Decor ✓	✓ Gear & Equipment
Nursing & Feeding ✗	✗ Safety & Babycare
Clothing, Shoes & Accessories ✓	✗ Books, Toys & Entertainment

usillygoose.com

Furniture, Bedding & Decor ✓	✗ Gear & Equipment
Nursing & Feeding ✗	✗ Safety & Babycare
Clothing, Shoes & Accessories ✗	✓ Books, Toys & Entertainment

walmart.com

"...the site is packed with information, which can be a little difficult to navigate... anything and everything you need at a huge discount... good idea to browse the site and research prices before you visit a store... my order was delivered well before the estimated delivery date... I've found cheaper deals online than in the store..."

Furniture, Bedding & Decor ✓	✓ Gear & Equipment
Nursing & Feeding ✓	✓ Safety & Babycare
Clothing, Shoes & Accessories ✓	✓ Books, Toys & Entertainment

participate in our survey at

maternity clothing

City of Cleveland

Fashion Bug

" *...not the hippest collection around, but the clothes are really cheap and perfectly presentable... basics like cropped pants and babydoll shirts... plus-sizes are a 'plus' in my book... sale prices are great... check the web for coupons...* **"**

Casual wear	✓	$$$ .... Prices
Business wear	✓	❸ .... Product availability
Intimate apparel	✓	❸ .... Customer service
Nursing wear	✓	❹ .... Decor

WWW.FASHIONBUG.COM

CLEVELAND—3780 ROCKY RIVER DR (AT LORAIN AVE); 216.476.3040; M-SA 10-9, SU 12-6; FREE PARKING

CLEVELAND—7997 EUCLID AVE (AT E 79TH ST); 216.229.2126; M-SA 10-9, SU 12-6; FREE PARKING

participate in our survey at

Suburbs – East Side

★★★★★

"lila picks"

★ Expecting In Style

★ Motherhood Maternity

Baby Depot At Burlington Coat Factory

"...a surprisingly good selection of maternity clothes at great prices... staff can be hard to find so be prepared to dig... cute pants, skirts and sets... I wouldn't have thought that their selection would be as good as it is... not much other than casual items, but what they have is pretty good..."

Casual wear	✓	$$	Prices
Business wear	✗	❸	Product availability
Intimate apparel	✗	❸	Customer service
Nursing wear	✗	❸	Decor

WWW.BABYDEPOT.COM

NORTH RANDALL—20801 MILES RD (AT RANDALL PARK MALL); 216.587.1743; M-SA 10-9, SU 11-6; PARKING LOT

Expecting In Style

"...if you're pregnant and in need of clothes, then this is the place for you... they have everything—casual clothes as well as formal dresses... prices are good especially considering the selection they have... a fun shopping experience—they help you celebrate that huge belly you're carrying around..."

Casual wear	✓	$$$	Prices
Business wear	✓	❸	Product availability
Intimate apparel	✓	❸	Customer service
Nursing wear	✓	❸	Decor

WWW.EXPECTINGINSTYLE.COM

PEPPER PIKE—30799 PINETREE RD (AT LANDER RD); 216.464.9020; M W F 10-5, T TH 12-4

Fashion Bug

"...not the hippest collection around, but the clothes are really cheap and perfectly presentable... basics like cropped pants and babydoll shirts... plus-sizes are a 'plus' in my book... sale prices are great... check the web for coupons..."

Casual wear	✓	$$$	Prices
Business wear	✓	❸	Product availability
Intimate apparel	✓	❸	Customer service
Nursing wear	✓	❹	Decor

WWW.FASHIONBUG.COM

GARFIELD HEIGHTS—4916 TURNEY RD (AT LANGTON AVE); 216.341.2023; M-SA 10-9, SU 12-6

Gap Maternity

❝...the styles are very modern and attractive... the clothes are reasonably priced and wash well... comfy yet stylish basics... they have a great online resource and you can return online purchases at the store... average everyday prices, but catch a sale and you're golden... sizes run big so buy small... always a sale going on where you'll find hip items for a steal... **❞**

Casual wear	✓	$$$	Prices
Business wear	✓	❸	Product availability
Intimate apparel	✓	❹	Customer service
Nursing wear	✓	❸	Decor

WWW.GAP.COM

BEACHWOOD—26300 CEDAR RD (AT BEACHWOOD PL); 216.831.1178

JCPenney

❝...competitive prices and a surprisingly cute selection... they carry bigger sizes that are very hard to find at other stores... much cheaper than most maternity boutiques and they always seem to have some sort of sale going on... an especially large selection of maternity jeans for plus sizes... a more conservative collection than the smaller, hipper boutiques... good for casual basics, but not much for special occasions... **❞**

Casual wear	✓	$$	Prices
Business wear	✓	❸	Product availability
Intimate apparel	✓	❸	Customer service
Nursing wear	✗	❸	Decor

WWW.JCPENNEY.COM

RICHMOND HEIGHTS—701 RICHMOND RD (AT RICHMOND TOWN SQ); 440.449.3800; M-SA 10-9, SU 11-6; PARKING LOT

Kohl's

❝...a small maternity selection but I always manage to find several items I like... our favorite shopping destination—clean, wide open aisles... not a huge amount of maternity, but if you find something the price is always right... the selection is very inconsistent but sometimes you can find nice casuals... best for the bare-bone basics like T-shirts, shorts or casual pants... **❞**

Casual wear	✓	$$	Prices
Business wear	✗	❸	Product availability
Intimate apparel	✗	❸	Customer service
Nursing wear	✗	❸	Decor

WWW.KOHLS.COM

HIGHLAND HEIGHTS—6245 WILSON MILLS RD (OFF HWY 271); 440.442.6300; M-SA 8-10, SU 10-8; FREE PARKING

Mimi Maternity

❝...it's definitely worth stopping here if you're still working and need some good-looking outfits... not cheap, but the quality is fantastic... not as expensive as A Pea In The Pod, but better quality than Motherhood Maternity... nice for basics that will last you through multiple pregnancies... perfect for work clothes, but pricey for the everyday stuff... good deals to be found on their sales racks... a good mix of high-end fancy clothes and items you can wear every day... **❞**

Casual wear	✓	$$$	Prices
Business wear	✓	❹	Product availability
Intimate apparel	✓	❹	Customer service
Nursing wear	✓	❹	Decor

WWW.MIMIMATERNITY.COM

BEACHWOOD—26300 CEDAR RD (AT RICHMOND RD); 216.292.0559; M-F 10-9, SA 10-7:30, SU 12-6

participate in our survey at

Motherhood Maternity ★★★★★

"...a wide variety of styles, from business to weekend wear, all at a good price... affordable and cute... everything from bras and swimsuits to work outfits... highly recommended for those who don't want to spend a fortune on maternity clothes... less fancy and pricey than their sister stores—A Pea in the Pod and Mimi Maternity... they have frequent sales, so you just need to keep dropping in—you're bound to find something good..."

Casual wear	✓	$$$	Prices
Business wear	✓	❹	Product availability
Intimate apparel	✓	❹	Customer service
Nursing wear	✓	❸	Decor

WWW.MOTHERHOOD.COM

BEACHWOOD—26300 CEDAR RD (AT BEACHWOOD PLACE MALL); 216.292.0559; M-SA 10-9, SU 11-6

RICHMOND HEIGHTS—691 RICHMOND RD (AT MONTICELLO BLVD); 440.449.8714; M-SA 10-9, SU 11-6

Sears ★★★☆☆

"...good place to get maternity clothes for a low price... the clearance rack always has good deals and their sales are quite frequent... not necessarily super high-quality, but if you just need them for nine months, who cares... good selection of nursing bras... I love the fact that they carry maternity wear in larger sizes—I got so tired of looking in those cutesy boutiques and then being disappointed because they didn't have my size... the only place I found maternity for plus-sized women..."

Casual wear	✓	$$	Prices
Business wear	✗	❸	Product availability
Intimate apparel	✓	❸	Customer service
Nursing wear	✓	❸	Decor

WWW.SEARS.COM

NORTH RANDALL—501 RANDALL PARK MALL (AT RANDALL PARK MALL); 216.587.6300; M-F 10-9, SA 10-6, SU 11-5

RICHMOND HEIGHTS—621 RICHMOND RD (AT RICHMOND MALL); 440.473.8300; M-F 9-9, SA 10-6, SU 11-6

Target ★★★★☆

"...I was surprised at how fashionable their selection is—they carry Liz Lange and other really cute selections... the price is right—especially since you'll only be wearing these clothes for a few months... great for maternity basics—T-shirts, skirts, sweaters, even maternity bras... best of all, you can do some maternity shopping while you're shopping for other household basics... shirts for $10—you can't beat that... not the most exciting or romantic maternity shopping, but once you see the prices you'll get over it... as always, Target provides the perfectly priced solution..."

Casual wear	✓	$$	Prices
Business wear	✓	❸	Product availability
Intimate apparel	✓	❸	Customer service
Nursing wear	✓	❸	Decor

WWW.TARGET.COM

BEACHWOOD—14070 CEDAR RD (AT WARRENSVILLE CTR RD); 216.416.0025; M-SA 8-10, SU 8-9; PARKING LOT

BEDFORD—22735 ROCKSIDE RD (AT NORTHFIELD RD); 440.232.2093; M-SA 8-10, SU 8-9; PARKING LOT

MAYFIELD HEIGHTS—1285 SOM CTR RD (AT MAYFIELD RD); 440.995.9300; M-SA 8-10, SU 8-9; PARKING LOT

Suburbs – West Side

★ ★ ★ ★ ★

"lila picks"

★ Motherhood Maternity

Baby Depot At Burlington
Coat Factory

"...a surprisingly good selection of maternity clothes at great prices... staff can be hard to find so be prepared to dig... cute pants, skirts and sets... I wouldn't have thought that their selection would be as good as it is... not much other than casual items, but what they have is pretty good... **"**

Casual wear	✓	$$	Prices
Business wear	✗	❸	Product availability
Intimate apparel	✗	❸	Customer service
Nursing wear	✗	❸	Decor

WWW.BABYDEPOT.COM

MIDDLEBURG HEIGHTS—6875 SOUTHLAND DR (AT W 130TH ST); 440.842.6808; M-SA 10-9, SU 11-6; PARKING LOT

Closets Consignment
Boutique

Casual wear	✓	✗	Nursing wear
Business wear	✓	✗	Intimate apparel

WWW.CLOSETSCONSIGNMENT.COM

ROCKY RIVER—1100 LINDA ST (AT LAKE RD); 440.333.5379; M-T F-SA 11-5, W-TH 11-8, SU 2-5; PARKING LOT

Fashion Bug

"...not the hippest collection around, but the clothes are really cheap and perfectly presentable... basics like cropped pants and babydoll shirts... plus-sizes are a 'plus' in my book... sale prices are great... check the web for coupons... **"**

Casual wear	✓	$$$	Prices
Business wear	✓	❸	Product availability
Intimate apparel	✓	❸	Customer service
Nursing wear	✓	❹	Decor

WWW.FASHIONBUG.COM

BROOKLYN—4780 RIDGE RD (AT RIDGE PARK SQUARE); 216.741.8594; M-SA 10-9, SU 12-6; FREE PARKING

PARMA—1846 SNOW RD (AT BROADVIEW RD); 216.398.0292; M-SA 10-9, SU 12-6; FREE PARKING

JCPenney

"...competitive prices and a surprisingly cute selection... they carry bigger sizes that are very hard to find at other stores... much cheaper than most maternity boutiques and they always seem to have some sort

participate in our survey at

of sale going on... an especially large selection of maternity jeans for plus sizes... a more conservative collection than the smaller, hipper boutiques... good for casual basics, but not much for special occasions... **"**

Casual wear	✓	$$		Prices
Business wear	✓	❸		Product availability
Intimate apparel	✓	❸		Customer service
Nursing wear	✗	❸		Decor

WWW.JCPENNEY.COM

NORTH OLMSTED—5100 GREAT NORTHERN BLVD (AT GREAT NORTHERN MALL); 440.779.8800; M-SA 10-9, SU 11-6; PARKING LOT

PARMA—7900 DAY DR (AT RIDGE RD); 440.845.7200; M-SA 10-9, SU 11:30-5:30; PARKING LOT

STRONGSVILLE—17177 ROYALTON RD (AT HOWE RD); 440.846.8419; M-SA 10-9, SU 11-6; PARKING LOT

Kohl's ★★★☆☆

"*...a small maternity selection but I always manage to find several items I like... our favorite shopping destination—clean, wide open aisles... not a huge amount of maternity, but if you find something the price is always right... the selection is very inconsistent but sometimes you can find nice casuals... best for the bare-bone basics like T-shirts, shorts or casual pants...* **"**

Casual wear	✓	$$		Prices
Business wear	✗	❸		Product availability
Intimate apparel	✗	❸		Customer service
Nursing wear	✗	❸		Decor

WWW.KOHLS.COM

FAIRVIEW PARK—3221 WESTGATE MALL (AT W 210TH ST); 440.356.1500; M-SA 8-10, SU 10-8; FREE PARKING

PARMA—6860 RIDGE RD (AT DAY DR); 440.884.2600; M-SA 8-10, SU 10-8; FREE PARKING

STRONGSVILLE—17555 SOUTHPARK CTR (AT ROYALTON RD); 440.572.4474; M-SA 8-10, SU 10-8; FREE PARKING

Motherhood Maternity ★★★★★

"*...a wide variety of styles, from business to weekend wear, all at a good price... affordable and cute... everything from bras and swimsuits to work outfits... highly recommended for those who don't want to spend a fortune on maternity clothes... less fancy and pricey than their sister stores—A Pea in the Pod and Mimi Maternity... they have frequent sales, so you just need to keep dropping in—you're bound to find something good...* **"**

Casual wear	✓	$$$		Prices
Business wear	✓	❹		Product availability
Intimate apparel	✓	❹		Customer service
Nursing wear	✓	❸		Decor

WWW.MOTHERHOOD.COM

NORTH OLMSTED—418 GREAT NORTHERN MALL; 440.716.0905; M-SA 10-9, SU 11-6

PARMA—8031 W RIDGEWOOD DR (AT RIDGE RD); 440.843.6739; M-SA 10-9, SU 11-6

Sears ★★★☆☆

"*...good place to get maternity clothes for a low price... the clearance rack always has good deals and their sales are quite frequent... not necessarily super high-quality, but if you just need them for nine months, who cares... good selection of nursing bras... I love the fact that they carry maternity wear in larger sizes—I got so tired of looking in those cutesy boutiques and then being disappointed because they* *didn't have my size... the only place I found maternity for plus-sized women...* **99**

Casual wear	✓	$$	Prices
Business wear	✗	❸	Product availability
Intimate apparel	✓	❸	Customer service
Nursing wear	✓	❸	Decor

WWW.SEARS.COM

MIDDLEBURG HEIGHTS—6950 W 130TH ST (AT SOUTHLAND SHOPPING CTR); 440.886.7500; M-F 10-9, SA 8-9, SU 11-5

NORTH OLMSTED—5000 GREAT NORTHERN MALL (AT GREAT NORTHERN MALL); 440.777.8070; M-SA 10-9, SU 11-5

STRONGSVILLE—17271 SOUTHPARK CTR (AT SOUTH PARK CTR); 440.846.3500; M-SA 10-9, SU 11-5

Target

66 *...I was surprised at how fashionable their selection is—they carry Liz Lange and other really cute selections... the price is right—especially since you'll only be wearing these clothes for a few months... great for maternity basics—T-shirts, skirts, sweaters, even maternity bras... best of all, you can do some maternity shopping while you're shopping for other household basics... shirts for $10—you can't beat that... not the most exciting or romantic maternity shopping, but once you see the prices you'll get over it... as always, Target provides the perfectly priced solution...* **99**

Casual wear	✓	$$	Prices
Business wear	✓	❸	Product availability
Intimate apparel	✓	❸	Customer service
Nursing wear	✓	❸	Decor

WWW.TARGET.COM

PARMA—6850 RIDGE RD (AT DAY DR); 440.842.9001; M-SA 8-10, SU 8-9; PARKING LOT

ROCKY RIVER—20001 CTR RIDGE RD (AT HAMPTON RD); 440.895.2600; M-SA 8-10, SU 8-9; PARKING LOT

STRONGSVILLE—18200 ROYALTON RD (AT PEARL RD); 440.238.9924; M-SA 8-10, SU 8-9; PARKING LOT

participate in our survey at

Lake & Geauga

★★★★★

"lila picks"

★Motherhood Maternity

Baby Depot At Burlington Coat Factory ★★★☆☆

"...a surprisingly good selection of maternity clothes at great prices... staff can be hard to find so be prepared to dig... cute pants, skirts and sets... I wouldn't have thought that their selection would be as good as it is... not much other than casual items, but what they have is pretty good... **"**

Casual wear	✓	$$	Prices
Business wear	✗	❸	Product availability
Intimate apparel	✗	❸	Customer service
Nursing wear	✗	❸	Decor

WWW.BABYDEPOT.COM

MENTOR—7980 PLAZA BLVD (AT ROUTE 20); 440.255.4077; M-SA 10-9, SU 11-6; PARKING LOT

JCPenney ★★★☆☆

"...competitive prices and a surprisingly cute selection... they carry bigger sizes that are very hard to find at other stores... much cheaper than most maternity boutiques and they always seem to have some sort of sale going on... an especially large selection of maternity jeans for plus sizes... a more conservative collection than the smaller, hipper boutiques... good for casual basics, but not much for special occasions... **"**

Casual wear	✓	$$	Prices
Business wear	✓	❸	Product availability
Intimate apparel	✓	❸	Customer service
Nursing wear	✗	❸	Decor

WWW.JCPENNEY.COM

MENTOR—7850 MENTOR AVE (AT GREAT LAKE MALL); 440.255.4461; M-TH 10-9, F 9-10, SA 8-10, SU 11-8

Kohl's ★★★☆☆

"...a small maternity selection but I always manage to find several items I like... our favorite shopping destination—clean, wide open aisles... not a huge amount of maternity, but if you find something the price is always right... the selection is very inconsistent but sometimes you can find nice casuals... best for the bare-bone basics like T-shirts, shorts or casual pants... **"**

Casual wear	✓	$$	Prices
Business wear	✗	❸	Product availability
Intimate apparel	✗	❸	Customer service
Nursing wear	✗	❸	Decor

WWW.KOHLS.COM

MENTOR—9581 MENTOR AVE (AT OLD JOHNNYCAKE); 440.354.5800; M-SA 8-10, SU 10-8; FREE PARKING

Motherhood Maternity

"...a wide variety of styles, from business to weekend wear, all at a good price... affordable and cute... everything from bras and swimsuits to work outfits... highly recommended for those who don't want to spend a fortune on maternity clothes... less fancy and pricey than their sister stores—A Pea in the Pod and Mimi Maternity... they have frequent sales, so you just need to keep dropping in—you're bound to find something good...* **"**

Casual wear	✓	$$$	Prices
Business wear	✓	❹	Product availability
Intimate apparel	✓	❹	Customer service
Nursing wear	✓	❸	Decor

WWW.MOTHERHOOD.COM

MENTOR—7850 MENTOR AVE (AT GREAT LAKE MALL); 440.974.7340; M-SA 10-9, SU 11-6

Sears

"...good place to get maternity clothes for a low price... the clearance rack always has good deals and their sales are quite frequent... not necessarily super high-quality, but if you just need them for nine months, who cares... good selection of nursing bras... I love the fact that they carry maternity wear in larger sizes—I got so tired of looking in those cutesy boutiques and then being disappointed because they didn't have my size... the only place I found maternity for plus-sized women...* **"**

Casual wear	✓	$$	Prices
Business wear	✗	❸	Product availability
Intimate apparel	✓	❸	Customer service
Nursing wear	✓	❸	Decor

WWW.SEARS.COM

MENTOR—7875 JOHNNYCAKE RIDGE RD (AT DEEPWOOD BLVD); 440.974.5500; M-F 10-9, SA 8-9, SU 11-6

Target

"...I was surprised at how fashionable their selection is—they carry Liz Lange and other really cute selections... the price is right—especially since you'll only be wearing these clothes for a few months... great for maternity basics—T-shirts, skirts, sweaters, even maternity bras... best of all, you can do some maternity shopping while you're shopping for other household basics... shirts for $10—you can't beat that... not the most exciting or romantic maternity shopping, but once you see the prices you'll get over it... as always, Target provides the perfectly priced solution...* **"**

Casual wear	✓	$$	Prices
Business wear	✓	❸	Product availability
Intimate apparel	✓	❸	Customer service
Nursing wear	✓	❸	Decor

WWW.TARGET.COM

WILLOUGHBY—440.975.1922; M-SA 8-10, SU 8-9; PARKING LOT

Lorain & Medina

★★★★★

"lila picks"

★ Motherhood Maternity

JCPenney ★★★☆☆

"...competitive prices and a surprisingly cute selection... they carry bigger sizes that are very hard to find at other stores... much cheaper than most maternity boutiques and they always seem to have some sort of sale going on... an especially large selection of maternity jeans for plus sizes... a more conservative collection than the smaller, hipper boutiques... good for casual basics, but not much for special occasions... **"**

Casual wear	✓	$$	Prices
Business wear	✓	❸	Product availability
Intimate apparel	✓	❸	Customer service
Nursing wear	✗	❸	Decor

WWW.JCPENNEY.COM

ELYRIA—4500 MIDWAY MALL (AT MIDWAY MALL); 440.324.5736; M-SA 10-9, SU 11:30-5:30; PARKING LOT

Kohl's ★★★☆☆

"...a small maternity selection but I always manage to find several items I like... our favorite shopping destination—clean, wide open aisles... not a huge amount of maternity, but if you find something the price is always right... the selection is very inconsistent but sometimes you can find nice casuals... best for the bare-bone basics like T-shirts, shorts or casual pants... **"**

Casual wear	✓	$$	Prices
Business wear	✗	❸	Product availability
Intimate apparel	✗	❸	Customer service
Nursing wear	✗	❸	Decor

WWW.KOHLS.COM

AVON—35906 DETROIT RD (AT CENTER RD); 440.937.4166; M-SA 8-10, SU 10-8; FREE PARKING

MEDINA—4095 PEARL RD (AT FENN RD); 330.722.1977; M-SA 8-10, SU 10-8; FREE PARKING

Motherhood Maternity ★★★★★

"...a wide variety of styles, from business to weekend wear, all at a good price... affordable and cute... everything from bras and swimsuits to work outfits... highly recommended for those who don't want to spend a fortune on maternity clothes... less fancy and pricey than their sister stores—A Pea in the Pod and Mimi Maternity... they have frequent sales, so you just need to keep dropping in—you're bound to find something good... **"**

Casual wear	✓	$$$	Prices
Business wear	✓	❹	Product availability

| Intimate apparel | ✓ | ❹ | Customer service |
| Nursing wear | ✓ | ❸ | Decor |

WWW.MOTHERHOOD.COM

AVON—35868 DETROIT RD (OFF MIDDLETON DR); 440.937.2213; M-SA 10-9,
  SU 11-6

Old Navy ★★★⯪☆

"...the best for casual maternity clothing like stretchy T-shirts with
Lycra and comfy jeans... prices are so reasonable it's ridiculous... not
much for the workplace, but you can't beat the prices on casual
clothes... not all Old Navy locations carry their maternity line... don't
expect a huge or diverse selection... the staff is not always
knowledgeable about maternity clothing and can't really help with
questions about sizing... they have the best return policy—order online
and return to the nearest store location... perfect for inexpensive
maternity duds... **"**

Casual wear	✓	$$	Prices
Business wear	✗	❹	Product availability
Intimate apparel	✗	❸	Customer service
Nursing wear	✗	❸	Decor

WWW.OLDNAVY.COM

AVON—35852 DETROIT RD (OFF MIDDLETON DR); 440.937.0223; M-SA 10-9,
  SU 11-6

MEDINA—1155 N COURT ST (AT ROUTE 42); 330.723.0470; PARKING LOT

Sears ★★★☆☆

"...good place to get maternity clothes for a low price... the clearance
rack always has good deals and their sales are quite frequent... not
necessarily super high-quality, but if you just need them for nine
months, who cares... good selection of nursing bras... I love the fact
that they carry maternity wear in larger sizes—I got so tired of looking
in those cutesy boutiques and then being disappointed because they
didn't have my size... the only place I found maternity for plus-sized
women... **"**

Casual wear	✓	$$	Prices
Business wear	✗	❸	Product availability
Intimate apparel	✓	❸	Customer service
Nursing wear	✓	❸	Decor

WWW.SEARS.COM

ELYRIA—4900 MIDWAY MALL (AT MIDWAY MALL); 440.324.1600; M-F 10-9,
  SA 10-6, SU 11-5

Target ★★★★☆

"...I was surprised at how fashionable their selection is—they carry Liz
Lange and other really cute selections... the price is right—especially
since you'll only be wearing these clothes for a few months... great for
maternity basics—T-shirts, skirts, sweaters, even maternity bras... best
of all, you can do some maternity shopping while you're shopping for
other household basics... shirts for $10—you can't beat that... not the
most exciting or romantic maternity shopping, but once you see the
prices you'll get over it... as always, Target provides the perfectly priced
solution... **"**

Casual wear	✓	$$	Prices
Business wear	✓	❸	Product availability
Intimate apparel	✓	❸	Customer service
Nursing wear	✓	❸	Decor

WWW.TARGET.COM

AVON—35830 DETROIT RD (AT AVON COMMONS); 440.937.4301; M-SA 8-10,
  SU 8-9; PARKING LOT

participate in our survey at

ELYRIA—240 MARKET DR (AT W RIVER RD); 440.324.1000; M-SA 8-10, SU 8-9; PARKING LOT

MEDINA—1015 N COURT ST (AT REAGAN PKWY); 330.722.7539; M-SA 8-10, SU 8-9; PARKING LOT

Portage & Summit

★★★★★

"lila picks"

★ Motherhood Maternity

Baby Depot At Burlington
Coat Factory ★★★☆☆

"...a surprisingly good selection of maternity clothes at great prices... staff can be hard to find so be prepared to dig... cute pants, skirts and sets... I wouldn't have thought that their selection would be as good as it is... not much other than casual items, but what they have is pretty good... **"**

Casual wear	✓	$$	Prices
Business wear	✗	❸	Product availability
Intimate apparel	✗	❸	Customer service
Nursing wear	✗	❸	Decor

WWW.BABYDEPOT.COM

CUYAHOGA FALLS—510 HOWE AVE (AT TALLMADGE RD); 330.920.4213; M-SA 10-9:30, SU 11-6; FREE PARKING

JCPenney ★★★☆☆

"...competitive prices and a surprisingly cute selection... they carry bigger sizes that are very hard to find at other stores... much cheaper than most maternity boutiques and they always seem to have some sort of sale going on... an especially large selection of maternity jeans for plus sizes... a more conservative collection than the smaller, hipper boutiques... good for casual basics, but not much for special occasions... **"**

Casual wear	✓	$$	Prices
Business wear	✓	❸	Product availability
Intimate apparel	✓	❸	Customer service
Nursing wear	✗	❸	Decor

WWW.JCPENNEY.COM

AKRON—1500 CANTON RD (OFF WATERLOO RD); 330.733.6227; M-SA 10-9, SU 12-5

AKRON—2000 BRITTAIN RD (AT CHAPEL HILL MALL); 330.633.7700; M-SA 10-9, SU 12-6

Kohl's ★★★☆☆

"...a small maternity selection but I always manage to find several items I like... our favorite shopping destination—clean, wide open aisles... not a huge amount of maternity, but if you find something the price is always right... the selection is very inconsistent but sometimes you can find nice casuals... best for the bare-bone basics like T-shirts, shorts or casual pants... **"**

Casual wear	✓	$$	Prices
Business wear	✗	❸	Product availability
Intimate apparel	✗	❸	Customer service

Nursing wear............................. ✗ .... Decor

WWW.KOHLS.COM

AURORA—7005 N AURORA RD (OFF PETTIBONE RD); 330.562.4055; M-SA 8-10, SU 10-8; FREE PARKING

STOW—4240 KENT RD (AT STOW-KENT SHOPPING CTR); 330.688.0386; M-SA 8-10, SU 10-8; FREE PARKING

Motherhood Maternity ★★★★★

"...a wide variety of styles, from business to weekend wear, all at a good price... affordable and cute... everything from bras and swimsuits to work outfits... highly recommended for those who don't want to spend a fortune on maternity clothes... less fancy and pricey than their sister stores—A Pea in the Pod and Mimi Maternity... they have frequent sales, so you just need to keep dropping in—you're bound to find something good... **"**

Casual wear	✓	$$$	Prices
Business wear	✓	❹	Product availability
Intimate apparel	✓	❹	Customer service
Nursing wear	✓	❸	Decor

WWW.MOTHERHOOD.COM

AKRON—2000 BRITTAIN RD (AT CHAPEL HILL MALL); 330.633.1531; M-SA 10-9, SU 11-6

FAIRLAWN—3265 W MARKET ST (NEAR MOREWOOD RD IN SUMMIT MALL); 330.873.2631; M-SA 10-9, SU 11-6

Sears ★★★☆☆

"...good place to get maternity clothes for a low price... the clearance rack always has good deals and their sales are quite frequent... not necessarily super high-quality, but if you just need them for nine months, who cares... good selection of nursing bras... I love the fact that they carry maternity wear in larger sizes—I got so tired of looking in those cutesy boutiques and then being disappointed because they didn't have my size... the only place I found maternity for plus-sized women... **"**

Casual wear	✓	$$	Prices
Business wear	✗	❸	Product availability
Intimate apparel	✓	❸	Customer service
Nursing wear	✓	❸	Decor

WWW.SEARS.COM

AKRON—2000 BRITTAIN RD (AT CHAPEL HILL MALL); 330.630.4700; M-SA 10-9, SU 11-6

Target ★★★★☆

"...I was surprised at how fashionable their selection is—they carry Liz Lange and other really cute selections... the price is right—especially since you'll only be wearing these clothes for a few months... great for maternity basics—T-shirts, skirts, sweaters, even maternity bras... best of all, you can do some maternity shopping while you're shopping for other household basics... shirts for $10—you can't beat that... not the most exciting or romantic maternity shopping, but once you see the prices you'll get over it... as always, Target provides the perfectly priced solution... **"**

Casual wear	✓	$$	Prices
Business wear	✓	❸	Product availability
Intimate apparel	✓	❸	Customer service
Nursing wear	✓	❸	Decor

WWW.TARGET.COM

AKRON—2400 ROMIG RD (AT ROLLING ACRES MALL); 330.745.0495; M-SA 8-10, SU 8-9

CUYAHOGA FALLS—449 HOWE AVE (OFF RT 8); 330.928.0014; M-SA 8-10, SU 8-9

FAIRLAWN—2801 W MARKET ST (AT MILLER RD); 330.865.9001; M-SA 8-10, SU 8-9

STOW—4200 KENT RD (AT STOW-KENT SHOPPING CTR); 330.688.5928; M-SA 8-10, SU 8-9

participate in our survey at

Online

babiesrus.com   ★★★★☆

"...their online store is surprisingly plentiful for maternity wear in addition to all of the baby stuff... they carry everything from Mimi Maternity to Belly Basics... easy shopping and good return policy... the price is right and the selection is really good..."

| Casual wear | ✓ | ✓ | Nursing wear |
| Business wear | ✓ | ✓ | Intimate apparel |

babycenter.com   ★★★★☆

"...it's babycenter.com—of course it's good... a small but well selected maternity section... I love being able to read other people's comments before purchasing... prices are reasonable and the convenience is priceless... great customer service and easy returns..."

| Casual wear | ✓ | ✓ | Nursing wear |
| Business wear | ✗ | ✗ | Intimate apparel |

babystyle.com   ★★★★☆

"...beautiful selection of maternity clothes... very trendy, fashionable styles... take advantage of their free shipping offers to keep the cost down... items generally ship quickly... I found a formal maternity outfit for a benefit dinner, bought it on sale and received it on time... a nice variety of things and they ship in a timely manner..."

| Casual wear | ✓ | ✓ | Nursing wear |
| Business wear | ✓ | ✓ | Intimate apparel |

bellablumaternity.com

| Casual wear | ✓ | ✓ | Nursing wear |
| Business wear | ✓ | ✓ | Intimate apparel |

breakoutbras.com

| Casual wear | ✗ | ✓ | Nursing wear |
| Business wear | ✗ | ✓ | Intimate apparel |

breastisbest.com   ★★★★★

"...by far the best resource for purchasing good quality nursing bras online... the site is easy to use and they have an extensive online fitting guide... returns are a breeze... since they are only online you may have to try a few before you get it exactly right..."

| Casual wear | ✓ | ✓ | Nursing wear |
| Business wear | ✗ | ✓ | Intimate apparel |

childishclothing.com

| Casual wear | ✓ | ✗ | Nursing wear |
| Business wear | ✗ | ✗ | Intimate apparel |

duematernity.com ★★★★☆

"...refreshing styles... fun and hip clothing... the site is easy to navigate and use... I've ordered a bunch of clothes from them and never had a problem... everything from casual wear to fun, funky items for special occasions... prices are reasonable..."

| Casual wear | ✓ | ✓ | Nursing wear |
| Business wear | ✓ | ✓ | Intimate apparel |

evalillian.com

| Casual wear | ✓ | ✓ | Nursing wear |
| Business wear | ✓ | ✓ | Intimate apparel |

expressiva.com ★★★★⯪

"...the best site for nursing clothes... prices are good and their selection is terrific... lots of selection on dressy, casual, sleep, workout and even bathing suits... if you're going to shop for maternity online then be sure not to miss this cool site... good customer service—quite prompt in answering questions about my order..."

| Casual wear | ✓ | ✓ | Nursing wear |
| Business wear | ✗ | ✓ | Intimate apparel |

gap.com ★★★★★

"...stylish maternity clothes delivered right to your doorstep... always something worth buying... the best place for functional, comfortable and affordable maternity clothes... classic styles, not too trendy... more available online than in a store... no fancy dresses but lots of casual outfits that are cheap, look good and I don't mind parting with them after my baby is born... easy to use site and deliveries are generally prompt... you can return them to any Gap store..."

| Casual wear | ✓ | ✓ | Nursing wear |
| Business wear | ✓ | ✓ | Intimate apparel |

japaneseweekend.com ★★★★☆

"...pregnancy clothes that scream 'I am proud of my pregnant body'... a must for comfy, stylish stuff... they make the best maternity pants which cradle your belly as it grows... a little expensive but I lived in their pants my entire pregnancy—I definitely got my money's worth... really nice clothing that just doesn't look and feel like your traditional pregnancy wear—I still wear a couple of the outfits (my baby is now 6 months old)..."

| Casual wear | ✓ | ✓ | Nursing wear |
| Business wear | ✓ | ✓ | Intimate apparel |

jcpenney.com ★★★☆☆

"...competitive prices and a surprisingly cute selection... they carry bigger sizes that are very hard to find at other stores... much cheaper than most maternity boutiques and they always seem to have some sort of sale going on... an especially large selection of maternity jeans for plus sizes... a more conservative collection than the smaller, hipper boutiques... good for casual basics, but not much for special occasions..."

| Casual wear | ✓ | ✓ | Nursing wear |
| Business wear | ✓ | ✓ | Intimate apparel |

lizlange.com ★★★★⯪

"...well-designed and cute... the real buys on this site are definitely in the sale section... cute, hip selection of jeans, skirts, blouses and

bathing suits... their evening and dressy clothes are the best with wonderful fabrics and designs... easy and convenient online shopping... practical but not frumpy styles—their web site made my maternity shopping so easy... **"**

Casual wear	✓	✗	Nursing wear
Business wear	✓	✗	Intimate apparel

maternitymall.com ★★★★★

"*...I had great luck with maternitymall.com... a large selection of vendors in all price ranges... quick and easy without having to leave my house... found everything I needed... their merchandise tends to be true to size... site is a bit hard to navigate and cluttered with ads... sale and clearance prices are fantastic...* **"**

Casual wear	✓	✓	Nursing wear
Business wear	✓	✓	Intimate apparel

mommygear.com

Casual wear	✓	✓	Nursing wear
Business wear	✗	✓	Intimate apparel

momsnightout.com

"*...for that fashionable-not-frumpy fancy occasion dress... beautiful store with gorgeous selection of dresses from cocktail to bridal... one on one attention... expensive but worth it...* **"**

Casual wear	✗	✗	Nursing wear
Business wear	✓	✗	Intimate apparel

motherhood.com ★★★★☆

"*...a wide variety of styles, from business to weekend wear—all at a good price... affordable and cute... everything from bras and swimsuits to work outfits... highly recommended for those who don't want to spend a fortune on maternity clothes... less fancy and pricey than their sister stores—A Pea in the Pod and Mimi Maternity... they have frequent sales, so you just need to keep dropping in—you're bound to find something good...* **"**

Casual wear	✓	✓	Nursing wear
Business wear	✓	✓	Intimate apparel

motherwear.com ★★★★⯪

"*...excellent selection of cute and practical nursing clothes at reasonable prices... sign up for their e-mail newsletter for great offers, including free shipping... top quality clothes... decent selection of hard to find plus sizes... golden return policy, you can return any item (even used!) you aren't 100% happy with... they sell the only nursing tops I could actually wear outside the house... cute styles that aren't frumpy... so easy... pricey but worth it for the quality... top notch customer service...* **"**

Casual wear	✗	✓	Nursing wear
Business wear	✗	✓	Intimate apparel

naissancematernity.com ★★★★★

"*...the cutest maternity clothes around... hip and funky clothes for the artsy, well-dressed mom to be... their site is easy to navigate... if you can't make it down to the actual store in LA, just go online... clothes that make you look and feel sexy... it ain't cheap but you will look marvelous and the clothes will grow with you... web site is great and their phone order service was incredible...* **"**

Casual wear	✓	✗	Nursing wear
Business wear	✓	✗	Intimate apparel

nordstrom.com ★★★☆☆

"...now that they don't carry maternity in stores anymore, this is the only way to get any maternity from Nordstrom... overpriced but nice... makes returns harder, since you have to ship everything instead of just going back to a store... they carry Cadeau, Liz Lange, Belly Basics, etc... nice stuff, not so nice prices... "

Casual wear .... ✓   ✓ .... Nursing wear
Business wear .... ✓   ✓ .... Intimate apparel

oldnavy.com ★★★★☆

"...since not all Old Navy stores carry maternity clothes, this is the easiest way to go... just like their regular clothes, the maternity selection is great for casual wear... cheap, cheap, cheap... the quality is good and the price is definitely right... frequent sales make great prices even better... "

Casual wear .... ✓   ✓ .... Nursing wear
Business wear .... ✗   ✗ .... Intimate apparel

onehotmama.com ★★★⯪☆

"...you'll find many things you must have... cool and very nice clothing... they carry everything from underwear and tights to formal dresses... you can find some real bargains online... super fast shipping... also, lots of choices for nursing and get-back-in-shape wear... "

Casual wear .... ✓   ✓ .... Nursing wear
Business wear .... ✓   ✓ .... Intimate apparel

showeryourbaby.com

Casual wear .... ✓   ✓ .... Nursing wear
Business wear .... ✗   ✓ .... Intimate apparel

target.com ★★★★☆

"...lots of Liz Lange at very fair prices... the selection is great and it's so easy to shop online—we bought most of our baby gear here and I managed to slip in a couple of orders for some maternity wear too... maternity shirts for $10—where else can you find deals like that... "

Casual wear .... ✓   ✓ .... Nursing wear
Business wear .... ✓   ✓ .... Intimate apparel

participate in our survey at

activities & outings

City of Cleveland

★★★★★

"lila picks"

★ Cleveland Children's Museum
★ Cleveland Metroparks Zoo

Cleveland Botanical Gardens ★★★★☆

"...an escape for parents and kids alike, fun for sunny days or snowy days... the glasshouse is overrated, but the Hershey Garden is unparalleled... don't miss the 'botanicool' backpacks packed with kids activities as they travel the museum (check temp in shade/sun; see how bees transport pollen, etc.)... bring a lunch and change of clothes for the water activities... the children's garden is truly one of the best things about Cleveland... it is an amazing place that kids will want to return to time & time again..."

Customer service..........................❹ $$..Prices
Age range.....................1 yrs and up
WWW.CBGARDEN.ORG
CLEVELAND—11030 E BLVD (AT FORD DR); 216.721.1600; CHECK SCHEDULE ONLINE; PARKING LOT

Cleveland Childrens Museum ★★★★★

"...a whole bunch of big preschool learning centers in one building... there is a farm, a water play area (complete with slickers to borrow to keep clothes dry), a bank, an arts center (with musical instruments and crayons and puppets), a grocery store (complete with cash registers and a large selection of foods from around the world), a bus, a car and more... they have a small area where people can eat... museum staff hold all sorts of programs, from story times to art activities... could be more aesthetically pleasing... dingy... excellent place to have a birthday party... free parking and a year long membership is not too expensive..."

Customer service..........................❸ $$..Prices
Age range.....................1 yrs to 8 yrs
WWW.CLEVELANDCHILDRENSMUSEUM.ORG
CLEVELAND—10730 EUCLID AVE (AT E 107TH ST); 216.791.7114; T 10-5, W 10-8, TH-SA 10-5, SU 12-5

Cleveland Metroparks Zoo ★★★★★

"...big zoo, big fun... lots of different activities throughout the year... we especially love the Rainforest in the winter!.. a wonderful place to visit for people of all ages... the aquarium area needs to be updated—it is very dark and small... the Australian Adventure is chock full of fun-from walking among kangaroos and wallabys to a petting zoo, a giant slide, camel rides and a train... look out for the big, big, big hill on the left side-with a double stroller it's a killer... free on Mondays to Cuyahoga county residents... parking is free... it's worth getting a

membership especially when you have little ones... you go anytime and stay as long or as short as you want... **"**

Customer service .... ❹ $$ .... Prices
Age range .... 1 yrs and up

WWW.CLEMETZOO.COM

CLEVELAND—3900 WILDLIFE WAY (AT FULTON PKWY); 216.661.6500; DAILY 10-5; FREE PARKING AVAIL

Cleveland Museum Of Art ★★★★☆

"*...gorgeous artwork... works for babies and kids that are old enough to NOT touch the art... plenty of places to rest and it's FREE!.. be sure to check out the web site for fun downloadable art activities.. best activity for the little ones is in June called 'Parade the Circle' around University Circle; it's a festive parade celebrating diversity with colorful costumes and huge floats... museum is best for older kids, including kids who like medieval times, as they have a workshop with knights who help you design your own armor...* **"**

Customer service .... ❹ $ .... Prices
Age range .... 1 yrs and up

WWW.CLEVELANDART.ORG

CLEVELAND—11150 E BLVD (AT BELLFLOWER RD); 216.421.7340

Cleveland Museum Of Natural History ★★★★⯪

"*...terrific exhibits... everything from dinosaurs to moon rocks... kids will enjoy getting close to the animals without having to be afraid of them... very manageable size for an afternoon outing... the planetarium is the best part... don't miss the hands-on exhibits and the discovery room... great outing for those cold Cleveland days... lack of eating facilities, but cool gift shop... family membership is $55...* **"**

Customer service .... ❹ $$ .... Prices

WWW.CMNH.ORG

CLEVELAND—1 WADE OVAL DR (AT E 105TH ST); 216.231.4600; M-SA 10-5, W 10-10, SU 12-5; PARKING LOT $5 FLAT RATE

Cleveland Music School Settlement ★★★★☆

"*...informal, but very well-led music and activity classes for babies and preschoolers... expensive, but by far one of the best programs around... parent participation is required for babies but not for older kids... all the teachers are highly accomplished musicians... very well-respected in the community and nationally... also has a preschool, day school, and a music therapy program... once a month on Sundays, it hosts a free 'Klassical Kids' concert, which my 2-year old adores... older ones can take anything from violin to harp... birth to 3 has music and movement classes...* **"**

Customer service .... ❹ $$$$ .... Prices
Age range ....3 mths and up

WWW.THECMSS.ORG

CLEVELAND—11125 MAGNOLIA DR (AT MISTLETOE DR); 216.421.5806; CHECK SCHEDULE ONLINE; FREE PARKING

Great Lakes Science Center ★★★★★

"*...huge and like a lot of science centers, and most of it's over the heads of really little ones... best for three years and up... my kids especially love the Polymer room and I love the free demonstrations... the IMAX shows are cool, but can be overwhelming... adults pay $9 and kids (over three) pay $7...* **"**

Customer service .... ❹ $$ .... Prices

Age range............... 12 mths and up

WWW.GLSC.ORG

CLEVELAND—601 ERIESIDE AVE (AT EAST 9TH ST); 216.694.2000; DAILY
9:30-5:30

HealthSpace Cleveland ★★★½☆

"...little tots probably aren't going to understand most of the exhibits,
but they are so well done that kids of all ages will get a kick out of
them... water, things to pull and pull, lots to touch—kids love this
place... for older kids it's actually educational... **"**

Customer service..........................❸ $$$...Prices
Age range.....................3 yrs and up

WWW.HEALTHSPACECLEVELAND.ORG

CLEVELAND—8911 EUCLID AVE (AT E 89TH ST); 216.231.5010; W-SA 10-
4:30, SU 12-4:30

Rocky River Stables ★★★★☆

"...ponies and horses are always popular in our house... we started
with the tour and now my daughter does the pony camp ($175/6
classes)... they also have a therapeutic riding program for kids with
special needs... great place for a birthday party for three year olds+...
there is also a trail for walking or strolling... pony camps for four to
seven year olds... also hosts horse jumping shows which are fun to
watch throughout the Cleveland area... **"**

Customer service..........................❹ $ ....Prices
Age range.....................3 yrs and up

WWW.VALLEYRIDING.ORG

CLEVELAND—19901 PURITAS AVE (NEAR VALLEY PKWY); 216.267.2525;
CHECK SCHEDULE ONLINE; FREE PARKING

Western Reserve Historical
Society ★★★½☆

"...the Western Reserve runs a bunch of cool facilities, including the
History museum, Crawford Auto-Aviation museum, and the Library...
don't miss the special exhibits—Dr. Seuss, Peanuts, all the favorites...
great fun and learning... **"**

Customer service..........................❸ $$...Prices
Age range.....................3 yrs and up

WWW.WRHS.ORG

CLEVELAND—10825 E BLVD (AT E 108TH ST); 216.721.5722; M-SA 10-5, SU
12-5; GENERAL PARKING $5

YMCA ★★★★☆

"...most of the Ys in the area have classes and activities for kids...
swimming, gym classes, dance—even play groups for the really little
ones... ... some facilities are nicer than others, but in general their
programs are worth checking out... prices are more than reasonable for
what is offered... the best bang for your buck... they have it all—great
programs that meet the needs of a diverse range of families... check
out their camps during the summer and school breaks... **"**

Customer service..........................❹ $$...Prices
Age range..................3 mths and up

WWW.YMCA.COM

CLEVELAND—15501 LORAIN AVE; 440.871.6885; CHECK SCHEDULE ONLINE

CLEVELAND—2200 PROSPECT AVE; 440.871.6885; CHECK SCHEDULE
ONLINE

Suburbs – East Side

★★★★★
"lila picks"

- ★ Heights Parents Center
- ★ Kindermusik
- ★ Public Library (Baby & Me)

Barnes & Noble   ★★★★⯪

"...wonderful weekly story times for all ages and frequent author visits for older kids... lovely selection of books and the story times are fun and very well done... they have evening story times—we put our kids in their pjs and come here as a treat before bedtime... they read a story, and then usually have a little craft or related coloring project... times vary by location so give them a call..."

Customer service .... ❹ $ .... Prices
Age range .... 6 mths to 6 yrs

WWW.BARNESANDNOBLE.COM

RICHMOND HEIGHTS—691 RICHMOND RD (AT RICHMOND MALL); 440.720.0374; CALL FOR SCHEDULE

WOODMERE—28801 CHAGRIN BLVD (OFF RT 2); 216.765.7520; CALL FOR SCHEDULE

Borders Books   ★★★★☆

"...very popular weekly story time held in most branches (check the web site for locations and times)... call before you go since they are very popular and get extremely crowded... kids love the unique blend of songs, stories and dancing... Mr. Hatbox's appearances are a delight to everyone (unfortunately he doesn't make appearances at all locations)... large children's section is well categorized and well priced... they make it fun for young tots to browse through the board-book section by hanging toys around the shelves... the low-key cafe is a great place to have coffee with your baby and leaf through some magazines..."

Customer service .... ❹ $ .... Prices
Age range .... 6 mths to 6 yrs

WWW.BORDERSSTORES.COM

BEACHWOOD—2101 RICHMOND RD (AT CEDAR RD); 216.292.2660; CALL FOR SCHEDULE

CLEVELAND HEIGHTS—3466 MAYFIELD RD (AT N TAYLOR RD); 216.291.8605; CALL FOR SCHEDULE

SOLON—6025 KRUSE DR (AT BAINBRIDGE RD); 440.542.9480; CALL FOR SCHEDULE

Cuyahoga County Public Library (Baby & Me)   ★★★★★

"...tons of locations... check out the web site to find the right story time for your kid, they have everything from baby lap sit to 3rd graders

reading groups... best of all, it's free... limited number... baby reading lasts about 20 minutes... my kids love to read and I think it is because we are always going to the library... way better than going to a toy store... 99

Customer service..........................**4** $ .... Prices
Age range.................. 6 mths and up
WWW.CUYAHOGALIBRARY.ORG/CLASSESPAGES/PROGRAMS_FORKIDS.HTM
BEACHWOOD—25501 SHAKER BLVD; 216.831.6868
BEDFORD—70 COLUMBUS RD; 440.439.4997
CHAGRIN FALLS—100 E ORANGE ST; 440.247.3556
GARFIELD HEIGHTS—5409 TURNEY RD; 216.475.8178
GATES MILLS—7580 OLD MILL RD; 440.423.4808
INDEPENDENCE—6361 SELIG DR; 216.447.0160
MAPLE HEIGHTS—5225 LIBRARY LANE; 216.475.5000
PEPPER PIKE—31300 CHAGRIN BLVD; 216.831.4282
SOLON—34125 PORTZ PKWY; 440.248.8777
SOUTH EUCLID—4645 MAYFIELD RD; 216.382.4880

Cuyahoga Valley Scenic Railroad ★★★★☆

66...train rides throughout the Cuyahoga Valley... they always have special theme rides during the holidays... a memory your kids will hold on to for a lifetime—especially if they're crazy-about-trains... not cheap, especially if you're taking a family of four... kids under two are free..Thomas the Tank Engine has visited most years with a festival atmosphere with all sorts of Thomas characters—it sells out quickly so buy tickets in advance... 99

Customer service..........................**5** $$$.. Prices
Age range.................. 3 mths and up
WWW.CVSR.COM
INDEPENDENCE—7900 OLD ROCKSIDE RD (NEAR CANAL RD); 440.526.7128;
  CHECK SCHEDULE ONLINE; FREE PARKING

Gymboree Play & Music ★★★★☆

66...we've done several rounds of classes with our kids and they absolutely love it... colorful, padded environment with tons of things to climb and play on... a good indoor place to meet other families and for kids to learn how to play with each other... the equipment and play areas are generally neat and clean... an easy birthday party spot... a guaranteed nap after class... costs vary, so call before showing up... 99

Customer service..........................**4** $$$.. Prices
Age range....................birth to 5 yrs
WWW.GYMBOREE.COM
BEACHWOOD—1980 S GREEN RD (AT COLLEGE RD); 216.291.9969; CHECK
  SCHEDULE ONLINE

Heights Parent Center ★★★★★

66...these guys have it all—music classes for my baby and Pilates for me... the inside play area was a savior this winter... lots of parenting classes... colorful and fun... it's a non-profit organization so prices are generally reasonable... discussion & support groups in a variety of topics from adoption to ADHD... drop-in sessions offer flexible playtimes every week... a good way to meet new parents... wonderful toy lending library... 99

Customer service..........................**4** $$.. Prices
Age range.................. 3 mths and up
WWW.HEIGHTSPARENTCENTER.ORG

CLEVELAND HEIGHTS—1700 CREST RD (AT MAYFIELD RD); 216.321.0079;
  CALL FOR SCHEDULE; PARKING AT SEVERN & STAUNTON RDS

Jewish Community Center

"...programs vary from facility to facility, but most JCCs have outstanding early childhood programs... everything from mom and me music classes to arts and crafts for older kids... a wonderful place to meet other parents and make new friends... class fees are cheaper (if not free) for members, but still quite a good deal for nonmembers... a superb resource for new families looking for fun..."

Customer service .... ❹ $$$ .... Prices
Age range ....3 mths and up
WWW.CLEVEJCC.ORG

BEACHWOOD—26001 S WOODLAND RD (AT RICHMOND RD); 216.831.0700;
  M-F 7:30-6

CLEVELAND HEIGHTS—3505 MAYFIELD RD (AT TAYLOR RD); 216.382.4000;
  M-F 7:30-6

Joseph Beth Booksellers

"...such an amazing bookstore, they always have superb recommendations for new books... story time on Tuesdays through Fridays are a perfect way to start the day... my kids love being in the midst of all the books and book lovers...great location for lunch, shopping and story time..."

Customer service .... ❸ $$$ .... Prices
WWW.JOSEPHBETH.COM

LYNDHURST—24519 CEDAR RD (AT LEGACY VLG); 216.691.7000; M-TH 9-10,
  F-SA 9-11, SU 10-8 ; PARKING LOT

Kindermusik

"...a wonderful intro to music and group play... well-trained professionals make it both educational and fun for all ages... we started with the mom & baby class and now my boy feels confident enough to play without me... they have hundreds of programs nationwide... class quality definitely varies from location to location, and teacher to teacher... different classes for different ages... singing, movement, dancing and rhythm—what's not to like?..."

Customer service .... ❹ $$$ .... Prices
Age range .... 2 mths to 7 yrs
WWW.KINDERMUSIK.COM

CHAGRIN FALLS—139 BELL ST (AT PHILOMETHIAN ST); 440.247.0876;
  CHECK SCHEDULE ONLINE; STREET PARKING

SHAKER HEIGHTS—2885 CTLAND BLVD (AT SHAKER BLVD); 216.991.1063;
  CHECK SCHEDULE ONLINE; STREET PARKING

Little Gym, The

"...a well thought-out program of gym and tumbling geared toward different age groups... a clean facility, excellent and knowledgeable staff... we love the small-sized gym equipment and their willingness to work with kids with special needs... activities are fun and personalized to match the kids' age... great place for birthday parties with a nice party room—they'll organize and do everything for you..."

Customer service .... ❹ $$$ .... Prices
Age range .... 4 mths to 12 yrs
WWW.THELITTLEGYM.COM

SHAKER HEIGHTS—20707 CHAGRIN BLVD (AT WARRENSVILLE CTR RD);
  216.752.9049; CHECK SCHEDULE ONLINE

Music Together ★★★★⯪

"...the best mom and baby classes out there... music, singing, dancing—even instruments for tots to play with... liberal make-up policy, great venues, take home books, CDs and tapes which are different each semester... it's a national franchise so instructors vary and have their own style... different age groups get mixed up which makes it a good learning experience for all involved... the highlight of our week—grandma always comes along... be prepared to have your tot sing the songs at home, in the car—everywhere... "

Customer service.........................❹ $$$...Prices
Age range................. 2 mths to 5 yrs
WWW.MUSICTOGETHER.COM

CHAGRIN FALLS—16349 CHILLICOTHE RD (AT WOODBERRY BLVD); 440.543.5025; CALL FOR SCHEDULE

CLEVELAND HEIGHTS—917.690.7365; CALL FOR SCHEDULE

SHAKER HEIGHTS—2860 COVENTRY RD (AT DREXMORE RD); 440.543.5025; CALL FOR SCHEDULE; STREET PARKING

SOLON—33955 SHERBROOK RD (AT RTE 91); 440.543.5025; CALL FOR SCHEDULE

My Gym Children's Fitness Center ★★★★☆

"...a wonderful gym environment for parents with babies and older tots... classes range from tiny tots to school-aged children and the staff is great about making it fun for all ages... equipment and facilities are really neat—ropes, pulleys, swings, you name it... the kind of place your kids hate to leave... the staff's enthusiasm is contagious... great for memorable birthday parties... although it's a franchise, each gym seems to have its own individual feeling... awesome for meeting playmates and other parents... "

Customer service.........................❹ $$$...Prices
Age range................. 3 mths to 9 yrs
WWW.MY-GYM.COM

SOLON—34304 AURORA RD (AT SOM CENTRAL RD); 440.914.9497; CHECK SCHEDULE ONLINE

Playground World ★★★⯪☆

"...at first, it may seem odd to play in a 'showroom', but don't let that stop you, it's just like going to a park—you don't have to buy anything... free play at the 'Play Zone' on weekday mornings at most of their locations... especially great in the winter... rainbow play sets, Victorian playhouses and log cabins... you can plan birthday parties here; it's also fun on summer days... "

Customer service.........................❹ $$...Prices
WWW.PGWORLD.COM

BEDFORD HEIGHTS—24206 AURORA RD (AT ROCKSIDE RD); 440.735.1188; M-TU 10-6, W 10-5, TH-F 10-6, SA 10-4, SU 11-4; PARKING LOT

Reel Moms (Loews Theatres) ★★★★☆

"...not really an activity for kids, but rather something you can easily do with your baby... first-run movies for people with babies... the sound is low, the lights turned up and no one cares if your baby cries... packed with moms changing diapers all over the place... so nice to be able to go see current movies... don't have to worry about baby noise... relaxed environment with moms, dads and babies wandering all over... the staff is very friendly and there is a real community feel... a great idea and very well done... "

Customer service.........................❹ $$...Prices
Age range................. 3 mths to 2 yrs

WWW.ENJOYTHESHOW.COM/REELMOMS

RICHMOND HEIGHTS—440.720.0500; CHECK SCHEDULE ONLINE

Shaker Family Center ★★★⯪☆

"...fun playroom with playstations... inexpensive... I recommend you get either a three month or one year membership... you don't have to live in Shaker Heights, but it is less expensive if you do... weekly discussion groups for new parents.. playroom for ages birth to three plus baby talk classes, stories, music and crafts... offers fairs about preschool and kindergarten readiness... "

Customer service .... ❸ $ .... Prices
Age range .... 9 mths to 5 yrs

WWW.SHAKERFAMILYCENTER.ORG

SHAKER HEIGHTS—19824 SUSSEX RD (OFF CHAGRIN BLVD); 216.921.2023;
   CHECK SCHEDULE ONLINE; FREE PARKING

Shaker Lakes Nature Center ★★★⯪☆

"...awesome classes, nature hikes, and bird walks in a beautiful setting... the classes are a blast—even if my baby doesn't always understand everything... learn about nature and animals... kids love it... bring some bread to feed the ducks in the pond... costs vary, but the membership is definitely worthwhile... adventure camps and classes for ages 2 1/2 to 10... nature walks and photography for adults too... "

Customer service .... ❸ $$$ .... Prices
Age range .... 2 yrs and up

WWW.SHAKERLAKES.ORG

SHAKER HEIGHTS—2600 S PARK BLVD (AT N WOODLAND RD);
   216.321.5935; M-SA 10-5, SU 1-5

Solon Arts Center ★★★★★

"...check out the mom and me music classes... singing and dancing for newborns on up... great teacher... wood floors so bring non-slip slippers for the new walkers... art, music, theater and dance—a wonderful resource for local families... Kindermusik of Cleveland uses this facility for its Solon teachers... everything from violin to acting to dance for the older kids... "

Customer service .... ❺ $$$$ .... Prices
Age range .... 12 mths and up

WWW.SOLONARTS.ORG

SOLON—6315 SOM CENTER RD (AT BAINBRIDGE RD); 440.337.1400; CHECK
   SCHEDULE ONLINE; FREE PARKING

Suburbs – West Side

★★★★★
"lila picks"

★ Memphis Kiddie Park
★ Public Library (Baby & Me)

Barnes & Noble

"...wonderful weekly story times for all ages and frequent author visits for older kids... lovely selection of books and the story times are fun and very well done... they have evening story times—we put our kids in their pjs and come here as a treat before bedtime... they read a story, and then usually have a little craft or related coloring project... times vary by location so give them a call... "

Customer service......................... ❹ $ .... Prices
Age range................. 6 mths to 6 yrs
WWW.BARNESANDNOBLE.COM
WESTLAKE—198 CROCKER PARK BLVD (OFF RT 2); 440.250.9233; CALL FOR
   SCHEDULE

Borders Books ★★★★☆

"...very popular weekly story time held in most branches (check the web site for locations and times)... call before you go since they are very popular and get extremely crowded... kids love the unique blend of songs, stories and dancing... Mr. Hatbox's appearances are a delight to everyone (unfortunately he doesn't make appearances at all locations)... large children's section is well categorized and well priced... they make it fun for young tots to browse through the board-book section by hanging toys around the shelves... the low-key cafe is a great place to have coffee with your baby and leaf through some magazines... "

Customer service......................... ❹ $ .... Prices
Age range................. 6 mths to 6 yrs
WWW.BORDERSSTORES.COM
PARMA—7793 W RIDGEWOOD DR (AT RIDGE RD); 440.845.5911; CALL FOR
   SCHEDULE
STRONGSVILLE—17200 ROYALTON RD (AT SOUTH PARK CTR OFF I-71);
   440.846.1144; CALL FOR SCHEDULE
WESTLAKE—PROMENADE OF WESTLAKE (AT CROCKER RD); 440.892.7667;
   CALL FOR SCHEDULE

Brecksville Community Center

"...beautiful community center with daycare... well maintained equipment, but baby area separated from older area... hard if you have a range of ages... easy place to meet up with other parents, especially on cold and rainy days... "

Customer service......................... ❹ $$... Prices
Age range..................... 1 yrs and up
WWW.BRECKSVILLE.OH.US

BRECKSVILLE—1 COMMUNITY DR (AT BRECKSVILLE RD); 440.546.2300; M-F
   6-10, SA 8-8, SU 10-5

Brecksville Stables

"...ponies and horses are always a big hit with our kids... we started
with the tour and now my daughter does the pony camp ($175/6
classes)... they also have a therapeutic riding program for kids with
special needs... great place for a birthday party for 3 year olds+... there
is also a trail for walking or strolling... pony camps for 4-7 year olds...
also hosts horse jumping shows which are fun to watch throughout the
Cleveland area... **"**

Customer service .... ❸ $$$ .... Prices
Age range .... 3 yrs and up
WWW.VALLEYRIDING.ORG

BRECKSVILLE—11921 PARKVIEW RD (AT WHISKEY LN); 440.526.6767;
   CHECK SCHEDULE ONLINE

Build-A-Bear Workshop

"...design and make your own bear—it's a dream come true... the
most cherished toy my daughter owns... they even come with birth
certificates... the staff is fun and knows how to play along with the
kids' excitement... the basic stuffed animal is only about $15, but the
extras add up quickly... great for field trips, birthdays and special
occasions... how darling—my nephew is 8 years old now, and still
sleeps with his favorite bear... **"**

Customer service .... ❹ $$$ .... Prices
Age range .... 3 yrs and up
WWW.BUILDABEAR.COM

STRONGSVILLE—320 SOUTHPARK CTR (AT WESTFIELD SHOPPINGTOWN
   SOUTHPARK); 440.878.1322; M-SA 10-9:30, SU 11-6

Cuyahoga County Public
Library (Baby & Me)

"...tons of locations... check out the web site to find the right story
time for your kid, they have everything from baby lap sit to 3rd graders
reading groups... best of all, it's free... limited number... baby reading
lasts about 20 minutes... my kids love to read and I think it is because
we are always going to the library... way better than going to a toy
store... **"**

Customer service .... ❹ $ .... Prices
Age range ....6 mths and up
WWW.CUYAHOGALIBRARY.ORG/CLASSESPAGES/PROGRAMS_FORKIDS.HTM

BAY VILLAGE—502 CAHOON RD (AT WOLF RD); 440.871.6392; CHECK
   SCHEDULE ONLINE

BEREA—7 BEREA COMMONS (AT S ROCKY RIVER DR); 440.234.5475; CHECK
   SCHEDULE ONLINE

BRECKSVILLE—9089 BRECKSVILLE RD; 440.526.1102

BROOKLYN—4480 RIDGE RD; 216.398.4600

FAIRVIEW PARK—21255 LORAIN RD (AT W 212TH ST); 440.333.4700; CHECK
   SCHEDULE ONLINE

LAKEWOOD—15425 DETROIT AVE (AT MARS AVE); 216.226.8275; FREE
   PARKING

MIDDLEBURG HEIGHTS—15600 E BAGLEY RD (AT BIG CREEK PKWY);
   440.234.3600; CHECK ONLINE OR SCHEDULE

NORTH OLMSTED—27403 LORAIN RD; 440.777.6211

NORTH ROYALTON—14600 STATE RD; 440.237.3800

OLMSTED FALLS—7850 MAIN ST; 440.235.1150

PARMA—2121 SNOW RD; 216.661.4240

PARMA—5850 RIDGE RD; 440.888.4300

PARMA—7335 RIDGE RD; 440.885.5362

PARMA HEIGHTS—6206 PEARL RD; 440.884.2313

STRONGSVILLE—18700 WESTWOOD DR (AT PEARL RD); 440.238.5530;
  CHECK SCHEDULE ONLINE

Ehrnfelt Recreation Center

"...like warm water?.. this is a fantastic pool for playing and learning how to swim... pirate ship and water slide... many classes to choose from—swimming, dance, gymnastics, arts and crafts... the staff varies from class to class, but overall we've always had a good experience... daycare on site if parents want to use the fitness facility... not cheap, but good value... open to members and non-members... check the calendar or call first to make sure the pool is open when you want to go... the downside is that there's no public outdoor pool facility anymore in Strongsville... "

Customer service..........................❹ $$$...Prices
Age range.................. 6 mths and up

WWW.STRONGSVILLE.ORG/CONTENT/FACILITIES.ASP

STRONGSVILLE—18100 ROYALTON RD (AT ORDNER DR); 440.878.6000;
  CHECK SCHEDULE ONLINE; FREE PARKING

First Chair Student Music Programs

"...a fun music and movement class... keeps my little one's attention... classes for babies to pre-schoolers... gets pricey, especially for two... also offers guitar, violin, voice, and piano to older ones ... "

Customer service..........................❹ $$$...Prices
Age range................ 12 mths and up

NORTH ROYALTON—13385 W 130TH ST (AT ROYALTON RD); 440.582.5878;
  CALL FOR SCHEDULE

Gymboree Play & Music

"...we've done several rounds of classes with our kids and they absolutely love it... colorful, padded environment with tons of things to climb and play on... a good indoor place to meet other families and for kids to learn how to play with each other... the equipment and play areas are generally neat and clean... an easy birthday party spot... a guaranteed nap after class... costs vary, so call before showing up... "

Customer service..........................❹ $$$...Prices
Age range.....................birth to 5 yrs

WWW.GYMBOREE.COM

STRONGSVILLE—15139 PEARL RD (AT STRONGSVILLE: STRONGSVILLE TOWN
  CTR); 440.878.4578; CHECK SCHEDULE ONLINE

Lake Erie Nature & Science Center

"...a relaxed place to go for the afternoon... my son never gets tired of going to see the turtles... we just started the weekly classes and love them, it's nice to have an easy destination... the center is free to visit, but you pay for the weekly classes... stroller-friendly hike... birthday parties here are a blast... offers a two-hour preschool class once a week... you can adopt an animal and the child gets a birth cerificate... planetarium has 'Twinkle Tots' show for $1 where kids watch lasers and lights dance and learn to enjoy the dark—on Thursdays and Saturdays at 11am... "

Customer service..........................❹ $$...Prices
Age range.................. 6 mths and up
WWW.LENSC.ORG

BAY VILLAGE—28728 WOLF RD (AT CLEVELAND METRO PARK);
440.871.2900; DAILY 10-5; FREE PARKING

Little Gym, The

"...a well thought-out program of gym and tumbling geared toward different age groups... a clean facility, excellent and knowledgeable staff... we love the small-sized gym equipment and their willingness to work with kids with special needs... activities are fun and personalized to match the kids' age... great place for birthday parties with a nice party room—they'll organize and do everything for you... **"**

Customer service .... ❹ $$$ .... Prices
Age range .... 4 mths to 12 yrs

WWW.THELITTLEGYM.COM

NORTH OLMSTED—24140 LORAIN RD (AT CURTIS DR); 440.734.4900;
CHECK SCHEDULE ONLINE

STRONGSVILLE—19748 W 130TH ST (AT HUNT & BENNETT RDS);
440.268.9008; CHECK SCHEDULE ONLINE

Memphis Kiddie Park

"...pay-as-you-go, kid-sized fun in a sweetly gaudy vintage setting... this is a must for anyone with kids between the age of 2 and 5... it is a great Cleveland tradition... I went as a child-now it's fun to go with my family!.. the staff is fabulous.. if your child starts to cry they will stop the ride so your little one can get off... very clean... open April through September... another good birthday party option... **"**

Customer service .... ❹ $ .... Prices
Age range .... 2 yrs to 5 yrs

WWW.MEMPHISKIDDIEPARK.COM

BROOKLYN—10340 MEMPHIS AVE (AT TIEDMAN RD); 216.941.5995; F-SA
10-9, SU-TH 10-8:30

Middleburg Heights
Recreation Center

"...one of the best outdoor and indoor pools on the west side... outdoor baby pool flows right into the big pool, which has sprays and large floating animals... limited nonresident summer passes are available, and they go quickly in the spring... a bonus is the reasonably priced indoor/outdoor childcare services so you can catch a workout on their new stair climbers and treadmills before heading to the pools... **"**

Customer service .... ❸ $$$ .... Prices
Age range .... 3 mths and up

WWW.MIDDLEBURGREC.COM

MIDDLEBURG HEIGHTS—16000 BAGLEY RD (AT BIG CREEK PKWY);
440.234.2255; CHECK SCHEDULE ONLINE

My Gym Children's Fitness
Center

"...a wonderful gym environment for parents with babies and older tots... classes range from tiny tots to school-aged children and the staff is great about making it fun for all ages... equipment and facilities are really neat—ropes, pulleys, swings, you name it... the kind of place your kids hate to leave... the staff's enthusiasm is contagious... great for memorable birthday parties... although it's a franchise, each gym seems to have its own individual feeling... awesome for meeting playmates and other parents... **"**

Customer service .... ❹ $$$ .... Prices
Age range .... 3 mths to 9 yrs

WWW.MY-GYM.COM

WESTLAKE—25016 CENTER RIDGE RD (AT KING JAMES PKWY);
440.892.9700; CHECK SCHEDULE ONLINE

Pump It Up ★★★★☆

"...huge warehouse type buildings filled with a variety of bounce houses and inflatable obstacle courses... colorful, padded slides and bouncers... the birthday party I went to was a blast—kids and adults were having way too much fun... they have an open gym a couple of days a week for $5 per tot—a great way to jump around and burn off some energy... $200-$250 for a really easy party that will have everybody smiling... "

Customer service........................❹ $$...Prices
Age range.................. 2 yrs to 12 yrs
WWW.PUMPITUPPARTY.COM
MIDDLEBURG HEIGHTS—7007 ENGLE RD (AT ENGLE LAKE DR);
440.234.7867; CALL FOR APPT

Rocky River Nature Center ★★★★★

"...FREE and fun... inside and out... we took a class here with Nora the Explorer and she was just great with the kids... even the adults had fun... there are animals, a giant indoor tree, books, and puppets... fun walks... programs such as 'Sunday Funday' are fun for little ones to explore nature with stories and hands-on activities... "

Customer service........................❹ $ ....Prices
WWW.CLEMETPARKS.COM
NORTH OLMSTED—24000 VALLEY PKWY (AT SHEPARD LN); 440.734.6660;
DAILY 9:30-5; PARKING LOT

Rocky River Public Library ★★★★★

"...this library is amazing... they have reading times for kids of all ages plus music... don't miss the large baby-friendly upstairs section... friendly staff is always welcoming kids...story time registration opens for Rocky River residents first, then open to non-residents... diverse programs include jugglers and a traveling zoo... "

Customer service........................❺ $ ....Prices
Age range.................. 6 mths and up
WWW.RRPL.ORG
ROCKY RIVER—1600 HAMPTON RD (AT REARVIEW AVE); 440.333.7610;
CHECK SCHEDULE ONLINE

Swim Of Things ★★★☆☆

"...swim classes all year long... day and evening classes... nice warm water... my daughter was so excited to get on the frog jump wall... small classes (3:1 ratio)... intimate setting... teachers are knowledgeable and committed... "

Customer service........................❹ $$$.......................................Prices
Age range.................. 6 mths and up
WWW.SWIMOFTHINGS.COM
NORTH ROYALTON—14386 RIDGE RD (AT ROYALTON RD); 440.237.0316;
CHECK SCHEDULE ONLINE; FREE PARKING

YMCA ★★★★☆

"...most of the Ys in the area have classes and activities for kids... swimming, gym classes, dance—even play groups for the really little ones... ... some facilities are nicer than others, but in general their programs are worth checking out... prices are more than reasonable for what is offered... the best bang for your buck... they have it all—great programs that meet the needs of a diverse range of families... check out their camps during the summer and school breaks... "

Customer service........................❹ $$...Prices

Age range ....3 mths and up

WWW.YMCACLEVELAND.ORG

LAKEWOOD—16915 DETROIT AVE (AT CORDOVA AVE); 216.521.8400; CHECK
  SCHEDULE ONLINE

WESTLAKE—1575 COLUMBIA RD (AT HILLIARD BLVD); 440.871.6885; CHECK
  SCHEDULE ONLINE

Lake & Geauga

★★★★★

"lila picks"

★Barnes & Noble

Barnes & Noble

"...*wonderful weekly story times for all ages and frequent author visits for older kids... lovely selection of books and the story times are fun and very well done... they have evening story times—we put our kids in their pjs and come here as a treat before bedtime... they read a story, and then usually have a little craft or related coloring project... times vary by location so give them a call...* **"**

Customer service......................... **❹** $ ....Prices
Age range................. 6 mths to 6 yrs
WWW.BARNESANDNOBLE.COM

MENTOR—7900 MENTOR AVE (OFF RT 615); 440.266.0212; CALL FOR SCHEDULE

Borders Books

"...*very popular weekly story time held in most branches (check the web site for locations and times)... call before you go since they are very popular and get extremely crowded... kids love the unique blend of songs, stories and dancing... Mr. Hatbox's appearances are a delight to everyone (unfortunately he doesn't make appearances at all locations)... large children's section is well categorized and well priced... they make it fun for young tots to browse through the board-book section by hanging toys around the shelves... the low-key cafe is a great place to have coffee with your baby and leaf through some magazines...* **"**

Customer service......................... **❹** $ ....Prices
Age range................. 6 mths to 6 yrs
WWW.BORDERSSTORES.COM

MENTOR—9565 MENTOR AVE (AT OLD JOHNNYCAKE); 440.350.8168; CALL FOR SCHEDULE

Build-A-Bear Workshop

"...*design and make your own bear—it's a dream come true... the most cherished toy my daughter owns... they even come with birth certificates... the staff is fun and knows how to play along with the kids' excitement... the basic stuffed animal is only about $15, but the extras add up quickly... great for field trips, birthdays and special occasions... how darling—my nephew is 8 years old now, and still sleeps with his favorite bear...* **"**

Customer service......................... **❹** $$$......................................Prices
Age range....................3 yrs and up
WWW.BUILDABEAR.COM

MENTOR—7850 MENTOR AVE (AT GREAT LAKES MALL); 440.205.8898; M-SA 10-9, SU 11-6; MALL PARKING

Gymboree Play & Music

"...we've done several rounds of classes with our kids and they absolutely love it... colorful, padded environment with tons of things to climb and play on... a good indoor place to meet other families and for kids to learn how to play with each other... the equipment and play areas are generally neat and clean... an easy birthday party spot... a guaranteed nap after class... costs vary, so call before showing up..."

Customer service .... ❹ $$$ .... Prices

Age range .... birth to 5 yrs

WWW.GYMBOREE.COM

MENTOR—9248 MENTOR AVE (AT MENTOR); 877.496.2644; CHECK
  SCHEDULE ONLINE

Karate For Kids

"...who would have thought a two year old could start karate (well actually, Taekwondo)... my little one loves the energy of the class and comes home happy and exhausted... the teachers are outstanding... combines the physical and mental-they are always working toward and meeting goals..."

Customer service .... ❺ $$$$ .... Prices

Age range .... 2 yrs and up

WWW.ATAONLINE.COM/ABOUT/PROGRAMS/KARATE.ASP

WILLOUGHBY—34601 RIDGE RD (AT MAPLEGROVE RD); 440.943.9999;
  CHECK SCHEDULE ONLINE; FREE PARKING

Playground World

"...at first, it may seem odd to play in a 'showroom', but don't let that stop you, it's just like going to a park—you don't have to buy anything... free play at the 'Play Zone' on weekday mornings at most of their locations... especially great in the winter... rainbow play sets, Victorian playhouses and log cabins... you can plan birthday parties here; it's also fun on summer days..."

Customer service .... ❹ $$ .... Prices

Age range .... 6 mths and up

WWW.PGWORLD.COM

CHESTERLAND—8035 MAYFIELD RD (AT HAROLD DR); 440.729.0909; M-F
  10-6, SA 10-5, SU 11-5; PARKING LOT

Lorain & Medina

★★★★★

"lila picks"

★ Avon Lake Public Library
★ Mapleside Farms

Avon Lake Public Library

❝...more than books... learning stations with all kinds of toys-magnets, music, and mirrors are just a few of the explorations... limited hours... beautiful space... huge play area for the kids that is science based... very kid friendly...hosts events like juggling shows and puppet shows and crafty Thursdays... story times during the week and Saturdays too... don't miss the outdoor alcove 'secret garden' next to the kids room... **❞**

Customer service........................❺ $ ....Prices
Age range.................. 6 mths and up

WWW.ALPL.ORG

AVON LAKE—32649 ELECTRIC BLVD (AT DRUMMOND RD); 440.933.8128;
CHECK SCHEDULE ONLINE; STREET PARKING

Borders Books ★★★★☆

❝...very popular weekly story time held in most branches (check the web site for locations and times)... call before you go since they are very popular and get extremely crowded... kids love the unique blend of songs, stories and dancing... Mr. Hatbox's appearances are a delight to everyone (unfortunately he doesn't make appearances at all locations)... large children's section is well categorized and well priced... they make it fun for young tots to browse through the board-book section by hanging toys around the shelves... the low-key cafe is a great place to have coffee with your baby and leaf through some magazines... **❞**

Customer service........................❹ $ ....Prices
Age range.................. 6 mths to 6 yrs

WWW.BORDERSSTORES.COM

ELYRIA—4333 MIDWAY BLVD (AT LORAIN BLVD & MIDWAY MALL);
440.324.5355; CALL FOR SCHEDULE

Little Gym, The ★★★★☆

❝...a well thought-out program of gym and tumbling geared toward different age groups... a clean facility, excellent and knowledgeable staff... we love the small-sized gym equipment and their willingness to work with kids with special needs... activities are fun and personalized to match the kids' age... great place for birthday parties with a nice party room... **❞**

Customer service........................❹ $$$......................................Prices
Age range................4 mths to 12 yrs

WWW.THELITTLEGYM.COM

AVON—2100 CENTER RD (AT DETROIT RD); 440.934.0494; CHECK
SCHEDULE ONLINE

Mapleside Farms

"...my family has been coming here for years... you can eat apples right off the trees... every year they have a Johnny Appleseed festival in September that is lots of fun for the whole family... they have crafts, game, a petting area for the kids, horse drawn wagon rides, and a corn maze... birthday parties and special holiday activities like breakfast with the Easter bunny, an October festival with pumpkins and a corn maze, and breakfast with Santa..."

Customer service .... ❹ $$ .... Prices
Age range ....6 mths and up
WWW.MAPLESIDE.COM

BRUNSWICK—294 PEARL RD (AT BEVERLY HILLS DR); 330.225.5577; CHECK
   SCHEDULE ONLINE; FREE PARKING

Playground World

"...at first, it may seem odd to play in a 'showroom', but don't let that stop you, it's just like going to a park—you don't have to buy anything... free play at the 'Play Zone' on weekday mornings at most of their locations... especially great in the winter... rainbow play sets, Victorian playhouses and log cabins... you can plan birthday parties here; it's also fun on summer days..."

Customer service .... ❹ $$ .... Prices
WWW.PGWORLD.COM

AVON—1014 JAYCOX RD (AT AVON COMMERCE PKWY); 440.937.5760; M-T
   10-6, TH-F 10-6, SA 10-4, SU 11-4; PARKING LOT

Portage & Summit

★★★★★
"lila picks"

- ★ Akron Zoo
- ★ Barnes & Noble
- ★ Hale Farm & Village

Akron Zoo ★★★★★

"...want an easy outing for little ones?.. this compact, well laid out zoo has all the favorites-lions and tigers and bears, oh my... not as overwhelming as the Cleveland Zoo... be sure to check out the special events such as Stroller Safari when the zoo opens extra early for kids birth to 2 and their families... every year we go to Boo at the Zoo and the snack with Santa... extra charges are worth it for pony rides, animal feedings (penguins in the winter), and train rides... **"**

Customer service.......................**❸** $$$.......................................Prices
Age range.................6 mths and up
WWW.AKRONZOO.COM
AKRON—500 EDGEWOOD AVE (NEAR BISHOP ST); 330.375.2525; CHECK
  SCHEDULE ONLINE; FREE PARKING

Barnes & Noble ★★★★★

"...wonderful weekly story times for all ages and frequent author visits for older kids... lovely selection of books and the story times are fun and very well done... they have evening story times—we put our kids in their pjs and come here as a treat before bedtime... they read a story, and then usually have a little craft or related coloring project... times vary by location so give them a call... **"**

Customer service.......................**❹** $ ....Prices
Age range................. 6 mths to 6 yrs
WWW.BARNESANDNOBLE.COM
AKRON—4015 MEDINA RD (AT N CLEVELAND MASSILION RD); CALL FOR
  SCHEDULE

Borders Books ★★★★☆

"...very popular weekly story time held in most branches (check the web site for locations and times)... call before you go since they are very popular and get extremely crowded... kids love the unique blend of songs, stories and dancing... Mr. Hatbox's appearances are a delight to everyone (unfortunately he doesn't make appearances at all locations)... large children's section is well categorized and well priced... they make it fun for young tots to browse through the board-book section by hanging toys around the shelves... the low-key cafe is a great place to have coffee with your baby and leaf through some magazines... **"**

Customer service.......................**❹** $ ....Prices
Age range................. 6 mths to 6 yrs
WWW.BORDERSSTORES.COM

AKRON—3265 W MARKET ST (AT SUMMIT MALL & MOREWOOD RD); 330.867.2601; CALL FOR SCHEDULE

AKRON—BRITTAIN RD (AT EVANS AVE); 330.633.2538; CALL FOR SCHEDULE

CUYAHOGA FALLS—335 HOWE AVE (AT MAIN ST); 330.945.7683; CALL FOR SCHEDULE

FAIRLAWN—SHOPS OF FAIRLAWN 3737 W (AT W MARKET & N CLEVELAND MASSILLION RD); 330.666.7568; CALL FOR SCHEDULE

STOW—4248 KENT RD (AT STOW-KENT SHOPPING CTR); 330.688.2184; CALL FOR SCHEDULE

Build-A-Bear Workshop ★★★⯪☆

66...design and make your own bear—it's a dream come true... the most cherished toy my daughter owns... they even come with birth certificates... the staff is fun and knows how to play along with the kids' excitement... the basic stuffed animal is only about $15, but the extras add up quickly... great for field trips, birthdays and special occasions... how darling—my nephew is 8 years old now, and still sleeps with his favorite bear... **99**

Customer service .... ❹ $$$ .... Prices
Age range .... 3 yrs and up
WWW.BUILDABEAR.COM

AKRON—3265 W MARKET ST (AT SUMMIT MALL); 330.864.2964; M-SA 10-9, SU 11-7; MALL PARKING

Geauga Lake & Wildwater Kingdom ★★★☆☆

66...fun, fun, fun... really little kids might not be able to go on some of the bigger rides, but there's plenty for the 'small' kids to do as well... choo choo train, foam factory, car rides... after enjoying rides, go to the water slides... special, shallow areas for tots... a fun family outing, especially if you have kids of varying ages... bring your own food—the concession stand is pricey and not that great... **99**

Customer service .... ❸ $$$ .... Prices
Age range .... 3 yrs and up
WWW.GEAUGALAKE.COM

AURORA—1060 N AURORA RD (AT GEAUGA LAKE RD); 330.562.8303; CHECK SCHEDULE ONLINE

Hale Farm & Village ★★★★★

66...I don't know who liked this more—me, my 4-year-old, or my 8-month-old... it's a farm where people still 'live and work' like it is 1860... you can watch glassblowing, blacksmithing and pottery making, spinning and weaving, candlemaking and basketmaking... horses, pigs, cows and sheep to keep the little ones happy... historical reenactments for the older set... especially fun and a nice day... $12 for adults and $7 for kids over 3... **99**

Customer service .... ❹ $$$ .... Prices
Age range ....6 mths and up
WWW.WRHS.ORG/HALEFARM

BATH—2686 OAK HILL RD (AT N CLEVELAND-MASSILON RD); 330.666.3711; CHECK SCHEDULE ONLINE; FREE PARKING

Jewish Community Center ★★★★☆

66...programs vary from facility to facility, but most JCCs have outstanding early childhood programs... everything from mom and me music classes to arts and crafts for older kids... a wonderful place to meet other parents and make new friends... class fees are cheaper (if not free) for members, but still quite a good deal for nonmembers... a superb resource for new families looking for fun... **99**

Customer service.........................❹ $$$..Prices
Age range.................. 3 mths and up
WWW.JEWISHAKRON.ORG
AKRON—750 WHITE POND DR (AT MULL AVE); 330.867.7850; M-F 7:30-6

Learned Owl Bookstore   ★★★★☆

❝...a cute community book store with a free story time event for toddlers... I love going to the Thursday 10:30am story time—my daughter sits on my lap and is enthralled by the story telling... they also have a wonderful kids department so you can pick up a gift or two... known for huge Harry Potter festivals when new books are released... store really gets involved with community events and works with schools and libraries to plan programs... **❞**

Customer service.........................❸ $$$..Prices
Age range................. 6 mths to 5 yrs
WWW.LEARNEDOWL.COM
HUDSON—204 N MAIN ST (AT AURORA ST); 330.653.2252; M-F 9-9, SA 10-9, SU 12-6

Little Gym, The   ★★★★☆

❝...a well thought-out program of gym and tumbling geared toward different age groups... a clean facility, excellent and knowledgeable staff... we love the small-sized gym equipment and their willingness to work with kids with special needs... activities are fun and personalized to match the kids' age... great place for birthday parties with a nice party room—they'll organize and do everything for you... **❞**

Customer service.........................❹ $$$..Prices
Age range................4 mths to 12 yrs
WWW.THELITTLEGYM.COM
FAIRLAWN—77 N MILLER RD (IN CROGHAM PK AT W MKT ST); 330.836.9609; CHECK SCHEDULE ONLINE
TWINSBURG—8922 DARROW RD (AT E AURORA RD); 330.405.9640; CHECK SCHEDULE ONLINE

Pump It Up   ★★★★☆

❝...huge warehouse type buildings filled with a variety of bounce houses and inflatable obstacle courses... colorful, padded slides and bouncers... the birthday party I went to was a blast—kids and adults were having way too much fun... they have an open gym a couple of days a week for $5 per tot—a great way to jump around and burn off some energy... $200-$250 for a really easy party that will have everybody smiling... **❞**

Customer service.........................❹ $$..Prices
Age range.................. 2 yrs to 12 yrs
WWW.PUMPITUPPARTY.COM
HARTVILLE—1135 W MAPLE ST (AT BIXLER AVE N); 330.877.7867

Step 2 Company   ★★★★☆

❝...headquarters of the playground, plastic car, and playhouse company is heaven for any toddler...factory has a retail store and trying out the products is welcome... salespeople aren't pushy...unfortunately, the discounted outlet is no longer there, so prices are full-ticket... worth the trip just to try out the products... limited hours... **❞**

Customer service.........................❸ $$$..Prices
Age range.................. 6 mths and up
WWW.STEP2COMPANY.COM
STREETSBORO—10010 AURORA-HUDSON RD (AT FROST RD); 330.528.0957; M-SA 10-5, SU 12-5

parks & playgrounds

City of Cleveland

★★★★★

"lila picks"

★Cleveland Lakefront State Park

Cleveland Lakefront State Park ★★★★★

"...so much to do, and over 400 acres... with the beach, boating, swimming, picnicking, bike and walking trails, concession stands, a playground, restrooms, and pets allowed, it makes for a great outing... there's also a scenic boardwalk, which is an added plus... "

Equipment/play structures............❸ ❸ ....Maintenance

WWW.COASTALOHIO.COM/SITE.ASP?ID=321

CLEVELAND—8701 LAKESHORE BLVD (AT ACCESS RD); 216.881.8141

Crossburn Playground ★★☆☆☆

"...not too much to do there... "

Equipment/play structures............❷ ❷ ....Maintenance

WWW.CITY.CLEVELAND.OH.US/GOVERNMENT/DEPARTMENTS/PARKSRECPROP/PRPREC/PRPRECPLAYGROUNDS.HTML

CLEVELAND—CROSSBURN (E OF W 130TH)

Estabrook Playground ★★★★☆

"...Estabrook Open Swim is one of our favorite activities... so nice to be able to go swimming in the middle of a Cleveland winter!... they also have other (free) activities for older kids... "

Equipment/play structures............❹ ❹ ....Maintenance

WWW.CITY.CLEVELAND.OH.US/GOVERNMENT/DEPARTMENTS/PARKSRECPROP/PRPREC/PRPRECPLAYGROUNDS.HTML

CLEVELAND—4125 FULTON RD (AT PARK RD)

Halloran Playground

WWW.CITY.CLEVELAND.OH.US/GOVERNMENT/DEPARTMENTS/PARKSRECPROP/PRPREC/PRPRECPLAYGROUNDS.HTML

CLEVELAND—3550 W 117TH ST (AT LORAIN AVE)

Impett Park Playground

WWW.CITY.CLEVELAND.OH.US/GOVERNMENT/DEPARTMENTS/PARKSRECPROP/PRPREC/PRPRECPLAYGROUNDS.HTML

CLEVELAND—W 155TH (AT MONTROSE)

Jefferson Park Playground

WWW.CITY.CLEVELAND.OH.US/GOVERNMENT/DEPARTMENTS/PARKSRECPROP/PRPREC/PRPRECPLAYGROUNDS.HTML

CLEVELAND—W 132ND (AT LORAIN)

Michael Zone Playground

"...a great wide-open space with plenty of room to run, but aging, inadequate play structures... look for a cutting-edge renovation of the entire grounds next year... **"**

Equipment/play structures .... ❶   ❸ .... Maintenance

WWW.CITY.CLEVELAND.OH.US/GOVERNMENT/DEPARTMENTS/PARKSRECPRO
P/PRPREC/PRPRECPLAYGROUNDS.HTML

CLEVELAND—6301 LORAIN AVE (AT W 66TH ST)

Suburbs – East Side

Beachwood Park ★★★★☆

"*...brand new park with great slides, swings, and teeter totters... right next to tennis courts and aquatic center with gigantic water slides... city's recreation center also sponsors carnivals, 'hands on trucks' day, 'bark in the park' for dogs, 'build a scarecrow' day, and many child enrichment classes...***"**

Equipment/play structures............**❸**   **❸**...............................Maintenance

WWW.BEACHWOODOHIO.COM

BEACHWOOD—25325 FAIRMOUNT BLVD (AT RICHMOND RD)

North Chagrin Reservation ★★★★☆

"*...beautiful areas of forestry, rivers, bicycling, bird watching, skiing, golfing, hiking, horseback riding, sledding, historical castle, visitor's center... a top spot for wildlife watching and picnic areas...***"**

Equipment/play structures............**❸**   **❸**...............................Maintenance

WWW.COASTALOHIO.COM/SITE.ASP?ID=128

GATES MILLS—ROGERS RD (AT CHAGRIN RIVER RD)

Roxboro Elementary School ★★★★☆

"*...there are a few child swings there, and lots of great slides and climbing toys... just don't go during recess, but weekends and afternoons are GREAT!...***"**

Equipment/play structures............**❹**   **❹**...............................Maintenance

WWW.CHUH.ORG

CLEVELAND HEIGHTS—2405 ROXBORO RD (AT JAMES PKWY); 216.371.7115

Turtle Park ★★★★★

"*...great place for babies and preschool age... fenced in and small enough that you can see them wherever they go... the playground equipment is nice—not too far to fall for the little ones—not much shade on a sunny day, though... great, safe place to play once they can walk...***"**

Equipment/play structures............**❹**   **❹**...............................Maintenance

CLEVELAND HEIGHTS—EUCLID HEIGHTS BLVD

Suburbs – West Side

Brecksville Reservation ★★★★☆

"...this vast, beautiful area of forests, farmlands, rivers and streams makes for an excellent outing, covering over 3,000 acres... there's a picnic area, barbecue grills, restrooms, a nature center, golfing, hiking, horseback riding.. lots of geological history and tons to see... ... **"**

Equipment/play structures .... ❸ ❸ .... Maintenance

WWW.COASTALOHIO.COM/SITE.ASP?ID=131

BRECKSVILLE—CHIPPEWA CREEK DR (AT STATE RTE 82)

Cuyahoga Valley National Park ★★★★★

"...great trails... lots of beautiful forestry makes walking and biking so enjoyable... **"**

Equipment/play structures .... ❸ ❹ .... Maintenance

WWW.NPS.GOV/CUVA

BRECKSVILLE—RIVERVIEW RD (AT VAUGHN RD)

Kauffman Park ★★★★☆

"...nice little playground, not too extensive, makes a nice stop before or after a library visit (located nearby)... a miniature golf course is at same site, as well as a baseball diamond... fully operational railroad tracks run nearby (separated by a fence) which is fun for kids who like trains... close to commercial district, but very nicely sequestered from traffic... **"**

Equipment/play structures .... ❹ ❹ .... Maintenance

WWW.CI.LAKEWOOD.OH.US/PW_PARKS.HTML

LAKEWOOD—5450 DETROIT AVE (AT W 55TH ST)

Lakewood Park ★★★★☆

"...lots of fun playground equipment, completely rebuilt in 2002, suitable for many ages... picnic pavilion, picnic tables, geese watching, .. beautiful Lake Erie view, and wide expanse of open field for running, playing sports, etc... lots of parents and kids running around, fence encircles most of playground, high visibility to most areas so it is easy for parents to socialize while letting kids run and play... movie programs in summer at small theater... Women's Pavilion hosts civic activities... tennis courts and swimming pool at park, skate park and scenic pier to be built... awesome park!... **"**

Equipment/play structures .... ❺ ❹ .... Maintenance

WWW.CI.LAKEWOOD.OH.US/PW_PARKS.HTML

LAKEWOOD—BELLE AVE (AT LAKE AVE)

Library Park ★★★☆☆

"...in the heart of Strongsville located behind the library... excellent all wooden playscape with bridges, beans, swings, slides, mirrors, musical pipes, balancing toys, tire toys, and plenty of up-and-down-and-over-and-around steps and plateaus... great place to play hide and seek... good for toddlers, but great for children 5-10... a couple of benches and areas for parents to sit and watch... very well maintained... sandy base... right next door to library, and down the road from tennis courts, baseball field, senior's center and rec center... by far the biggest playground area in Strongsville... **"**

Equipment/play structures .... ❹ ❹ .... Maintenance

WWW.CITY-DATA.COM/CITY/STRONGSVILLE-OHIO.HTML

Rocky River Reservation

"...*beautiful scenic rivers, forestry, lots of interesting geological history, picnic areas with grills, restrooms, gift shop, visitor center, biking, bird watching, golfing, canoeing, fishing, hiking, ice skating, kayaking, horseback riding... tons to do and see...* **"**

Equipment/play structures............ ❸   ❸ ....Maintenance

WWW.COASTALOHIO.COM/SITE.ASP?ID=256

NORTH OLMSTED—24000 VALLEY PKWY (AT CEDAR POINT RD);
   216.351.6300

Volunteer Park

"...*this is a nice park for a cooler day... the downside to this park is that there are no big trees around the playground area... once the small trees grow up around it, this will be a great park... one of our favorite parks; seldom crowded unless there is a baseball game (multiple baseball fields in the compound); beautiful wooded area with hill and ravine in viewing area, simulated rock climbing area, lots of bridges and overpasses to play on, several slides, and swing sets... good for toddlers, but great for older children...* **"**

Equipment/play structures............ ❹   ❹ ....Maintenance

STRONGSVILLE—21400 W LUNN RD (OFF FOLTZ INDUSTRIAL PKWY)

Wagar Park

"...*busy traffic nearby with no separation from playground (i.e. fences, hedgerows, et cetera)... older equipment... mostly used by residents within walking distance, as there's no parking or kid-friendly amenities nearby... never crowded...* **"**

Equipment/play structures............ ❷   ❷ ....Maintenance

WWW.CI.LAKEWOOD.OH.US/PW_PARKS.HTML

LAKEWOOD—15900 MADISON (AT HILLIARD BLVD)

Lake & Geauga

★★★★★
"lila picks"

★ Lake Farmpark

Holden Arboretum

★★★☆☆

"...great place to teach children about plants, flowers, etc... more geared for 3+ years... The Holden Arboretum connects people with nature for inspiration and enjoyment, fosters learning and promotes conservation... **"**

Equipment/play structures .... ❸ ❸ .... Maintenance

WWW.HOLDENARB.ORG

WILLOUGHBY—9500 SPERRY RD; 440.946.4400

Lake Farmpark

★★★★★

"...Lake Farmpark is a fun place to take children and adults alike... it's a working farm with all sorts of things to see, from horses, cows (and milking) to dogs herding sheep... there's a wonderful playground and picnic area in the front of the park that you can use for free... farming, wildlife, and nature programs... everything from watching how to make maple syrup to milking cows and running through a corn maze ... **"**

Equipment/play structures .... ❹ ❹ .... Maintenance

WWW.LAKEMETROPARKS.COM

KIRTLAND—8800 CHARDON RD; 440.256.2122

Penitentiary Glen Reservation

★★★☆☆

"...picnic area with grills, restrooms, hiking trails, cross-country skiing, Nature Center, Wildlife Center, Nature Connection Gift Shop, and a bridle trail... also provides birthday parties for ages 3-8... **"**

Equipment/play structures .... ❸ ❸ .... Maintenance

WWW.LAKEMETROPARKS.COM

KIRTLAND—8668 KIRTLAND-CHARDON RD (AT BOOTH RD); 440.256.1404

Lorain & Medina

★★★★★

"lila picks"

★ Hinckley Reservation

French Creek Reservation

WWW.LORAINCOUNTYMETROPARKS.COM/FRENCH.HTM

SHEFFIELD VILLAGE—4530 COLORADO AVE (AT ORCHARD CT); 440.949.5200

Hinckley Reservation

"...*this reservation, over 2,000 acres, has so much to see, from the wildlife, to the carvings, to the streams and geological formations that tell about the park's past... biking, birding hot spots, nature hiking, ice skating, kayaking, sledding, swimming, fishing, canoeing, barbecuing, picnic areas, an outdoor swimming pool and a lake, restrooms... there's something for everyone...* **"**

Equipment/play structures............**❺**　　**❺**..............................Maintenance

WWW.COASTALOHIO.COM/SITE.ASP?ID=285

HINCKLEY—LEDGE RD (AT KELLOGG RD); 216.351.6300

Portage & Summit

Little Turtle Pond
WWW.DNR.STATE.OH.US/WILDLIFE/FISHING/TROUT/DIRECTIONS_SPR.HTM
AKRON—2400 HARRINGTON RD (AT FIRESTONE METRO PARK)

restaurants

City of Cleveland

★★★★★

"lila picks"

★ Great Lakes Brewing Co
★ Yours Truly Restaurant

Anatolia Cafe

Children's menu.......................... ✓ ✗ .... Changing station
Highchairs/boosters .... ✓

WWW.ANATOLIACAFE.COM

CLEVELAND—13915 CEDAR RD (AT WARRENSVILLE CTR RD); 216.321.4400;
M-TH 11-10, F 11-10:30, SA 12-10:30, SU 12-10

Frank & Pauly's Banquet & Conference Rooms   ★★★☆☆

❝...one of the more kid-friendly places downtown... huge portions in this downtown favorite... loud environment makes it OK to bring the little ones... food is family style...what little one can say no to spaghetti?... ❞

Children's menu.......................... ✓ $$$.. Prices
Changing station .... ✗ ❹ ....Customer service
Highchairs/boosters .... ✓ ❸ .... Stroller access

WWW.FRANKANDPAULYS.COM

CLEVELAND—200 PUBLIC SQ (AT SUPERIOR); 216.579.1000; M-F 11:30-10,
SA 4-10:30, SU 5-8; BP PARKING GARAGE

Great Lakes Brewing Co   ★★★★★

❝...I never thought a brewpub could be so baby-friendly, but the staff is great, there's lots to look at, and the food is very good... cozy and smoke-free... kids may be most comfortable on the fenced patio... stroller access in this historic building isn't great, so pick that baby up... ❞

Children's menu.......................... ✗ $$$.. Prices
Changing station .... ✗ ❹ ....Customer service
Highchairs/boosters .... ✗ ❸ .... Stroller access

WWW.GREATLAKESBREWING.COM

CLEVELAND—2516 MARKET AVE (AT W 25TH ST); 216.771.4404; M-TH
11:30-10:30, F-SA 11:30-11:30, SU 4-9

Hard Rock Cafe   ★★★½☆

❝...fun and tasty if you can get in... the lines can be horrendous so be sure to check in with them first... a good spot if you have tots in tow—food tastes good and the staff is clearly used to messy eaters... hectic and loud... fun for adults as well as kids... ❞

Children's menu.......................... ✓ $$$.. Prices
Changing station .... ✓ ❹ ....Customer service
Highchairs/boosters .... ✓ ❸ .... Stroller access

CLEVELAND—230 W HURON RD (AT 2ND ST); 216.830.7625; SU-TH 11-11, F-SA 11-12AM

Johnny Mango

"...smokefree unique ambience with yummy food and drinks, including a juice bar... truly a 'world café'... every month has a new theme.. open for lunch and dinner, brunch on weekends... kids are certainly welcome and mine loves the quesadillas... **"**

Children's menu	✓	$$	Prices
Changing station	✗	❺	Customer service
Highchairs/boosters	✓	❹	Stroller access

WWW.JMANGO.COM

CLEVELAND—3120 BRIDGE AVE (AT FULTON RD); 216.575.1919; M-TH 11-10, F 11-11, SA 9-11, SU 9-10

Sergio's In University Circle

Children's menu	✓	✗	Changing station
Highchairs/boosters	✓		

WWW.SERGIOSINTHECIRCLE.COM

CLEVELAND—1903 FORD DR (AT EUCLID AVE); 216.231.1234; M-TH 5-9:30, F-SA 5-11

Yours Truly Restaurant ★★★★★

"...a very nice place for family dining... it's easy to fit strollers, highchairs, child seats, etc... good burgers, fries and other grilled items... one of my family's favorite places to eat... good, basic comfort food—an easy night out... **"**

Children's menu	✗	$$	Prices
Changing station	✓	❹	Customer service
Highchairs/boosters	✓	❹	Stroller access

WWW.YTR.COM

CLEVELAND—13228 SHAKER SQ (AT SHAKER BLVD); 216.751.8646; M-SA 6:30-11, SU 7:30-9; STREET PARKING

restaurants

Suburbs – East Side

★★★★★
"lila picks"

- ★ Benihana
- ★ Buca Di Beppo
- ★ Ruby Tuesday
- ★ Yours Truly Restaurant

Aladdin's Eatery

"...excellent Mediterranean food—the spinach pie is the best I've had, and their desserts are just amazing... you can order a side order of a veggie plate for the little ones (it has rice, carrots, peas, chick peas, beans)... yummy—lots of fresh squeezed juices... **"**

Children's menu	✓	$	Prices
Changing station	✗	❹	Customer service
Highchairs/boosters	✓	❹	Stroller access

WWW.ALADDINSEATERY.COM

CLEVELAND HEIGHTS—12447 CEDAR RD (AT FAIRMOUNT BLVD); 216.932.4333; SU-TH 11-10:30, F-SA 11-11:30, SU 11-10

Bahama Breeze

Children's menu	✓	✓	Changing station
Highchairs/boosters	✓		

WWW.BAHAMABREEZE.COM

ORANGE VILLAGE—2800 ORANGE PL (OFF RT 422); 216.896.9081; SU-TH 11-12, F-SA 11-1

BD's Mongolian BBQ

Children's menu	✓	✓	Changing station
Highchairs/boosters	✓		

WWW.BDSMONGOLIANBARBEQUE.COM

CLEVELAND HEIGHTS—1854 COVENTRY RD (AT EUCLID HEIGHTS BLVD); 216.932.1185; SU-TH 11-10, F-SA 11-11

Benihana ★★★★★

"...stir-fry meals are always prepared in front of you—it keeps everyone entertained, parents and kids alike... chefs often perform especially for the little ones... tables sit about 10 people, so it encourages talking with other diners... tend to be pretty loud so it's pretty family friendly... delicious for adults and fun for kids... **"**

Children's menu	✗	$$$	Prices
Changing station	✓	❹	Customer service
Highchairs/boosters	✓	❸	Stroller access

WWW.BENIHANA.COM

BEACHWOOD—23611 CHAGRIN BLVD (AT OLD GREEN RD); 216.464.7575; M-F 11:30-1:30, SA-SU 1-2:30, M-TH 5:30-9:30, F 5:30-10, SA 4-10, SU 4-8:30

Brennan's Colony

"...used to be known as only a john carroll bar, now they cater to dinner for little ones and their parents... burgers are terrific... still a bar so be sure to go early to miss the college crowd... video games for the older kids... **"**

Children's menu	✓	$$	Prices
Changing station	✗	❸	Customer service
Highchairs/boosters	✓	❹	Stroller access

CLEVELAND HEIGHTS—2299 LEE RD (AT SILSBY RD); 216.371.1010; SU-M 5-11, T-W 11:30-11, TH-SA 11:30-12

Buca di Beppo

"...massive Italian portions make this a great deal of a meal... entertaining atmosphere and attitiude... typically loud so crying little ones won't even be heard... be sure to share the meals and be ready for a doggy bag... **"**

Children's menu	✗	$$$	Prices
Changing station	✗	❹	Customer service
Highchairs/boosters	✓	❸	Stroller access

WWW.BUCADIBEPPO.COM

MAYFIELD HEIGHTS—1541 GOLDEN GATE PLZ (AT GOLDEN GATE MALL); 440.995.5550; M-TH 5-10, F 5-11, SA 12-11, SU 12-9

Cheesecake Factory, The

"...although their cheesecake is good, we come here for the kid-friendly atmosphere and selection of good food... eclectic menu has something for everyone... they will bring your tot a plate of yogurt, cheese, bananas and bread free of charge... we love how flexible they are—they'll make whatever my kids want... lots of mommies here... always fun and always crazy... no real kids menu, but the pizza is great to share... waits can be really long... **"**

Children's menu	✗	$$$	Prices
Changing station	✓	❹	Customer service
Highchairs/boosters	✓	❸	Stroller access

WWW.THECHEESECAKEFACTORY.COM

LYNDHURST—24265 CEDAR RD (AT RICHMOND RD); 216.691.3387; M-TH 11:30-11, F-SA 11:30-12:30, SU 10-11; MALL PARKING

Cici's Pizza

"...a great buffet for easy dining with kids... pizza at the right price... kids 3 and under eat free... very crowded during lunch and dinner rushes... not much room for strollers, but they'll help you find a place to stash it... they always have birthday parties and it's usually very crowded and noisy... pizza, pasta and salad buffet for under $10... **"**

Children's menu	✓	$	Prices
Changing station	✓	❹	Customer service
Highchairs/boosters	✓	❹	Stroller access

WWW.CICISPIZZA.COM

SHAKER HEIGHTS—16853 CHAGRIN BLVD (AT LEE RD); 216.751.3102; SU-TH 11-10, F-SA 11-11

Hoggy's Barn & Grille

Children's menu	✓	✓	Changing station
Highchairs/boosters	✓		

WWW.HOGGYS.COM

VALLEY VIEW—5975 CANAL RD (AT BRECKSVILLE RD); 216.328.9871; SU-TH 11-10, F-SA 11-11

J. Alexander's ★★★★☆

"...generous portions... burgers to die for... delicious salads... welcoming to youngsters and grown-ups alike... **"**

Children's menu......................✓	$$$..Prices
Changing station ....✓	❸ ....Customer service
Highchairs/boosters..................✓	❸ ....Stroller access

WWW.JASLEXANDERS.COM

LYNDHURST—5845 LANDERBROOK CIR (AT CEDAR RD); 440.449.9131; M-TH 11:30-11, F-SA 11:30-12, SU 12-10

Longhorn Steakhouse ★★★★☆

"...for meat and seafood lovers... the staff totally gets 'the kid thing' here... they bring out snacks, get the orders going quickly, and frequently check back for things like new spoons and napkins... lots of things for baby to look at... get there early or call ahead to avoid the wait... **"**

Children's menu......................✓	$$$..Prices
Changing station ....✓	❹ ....Customer service
Highchairs/boosters..................✓	❸ ....Stroller access

WWW.LONGHORNSTEAKHOUSE.COM

INDEPENDENCE—4171 ROCKSIDE RD (OFF RT 77); 216.642.8700; SU-TH 11-10, F-SA 11-11

SOLON—6015 ENTERPRISE PKY (AT COCHRAN RD); 440.498.9553; SU-TH 11-10, F-SA 11-11

Original Pancake House ★★★★½

"...consistently the best breakfast around... great flapjacks and appropriately-sized kids meals... food comes quickly... the most amazing apple pancakes ever... service is always friendly, but sometimes it can take a while to actually get the food... the highlight for my daughter is the free balloon when we leave... always a lot of families here with small children on the weekends, so you don't have to worry about being the only one... **"**

Children's menu......................✓	$$..Prices
Changing station ....✓	❹ ....Customer service
Highchairs/boosters..................✓	❸ ....Stroller access

WWW.ORIGINALPANCAKEHOUSE.COM

WOODMERE—28700 CHAGRIN BLVD (AT BELMONT RD); 216.292.7777; M-F 7-2, SA-SU 7-3

Pizzazz Pizza ★★★☆☆

"...in the heart of university heights across from john carroll... filled with college students, professors and young families... pizzas and salads are among the best in the area... parking is easy, but many locals can walk to pizzazz... **"**

Children's menu......................✗	$$$..Prices
Changing station ....✗	❸ ....Customer service
Highchairs/boosters..................✓	❸ ....Stroller access

WWW.PIZZAZZPIZZA.COM

UNIVERSITY HEIGHTS—20680 N PARK BLVD (OFF FAIRMOUNT BLVD); 216.321.7272; SU-TH 11-10, F-SA 11-10:30

Quaker Steak and Lube ★★★☆☆

"...a great place to bring the kids... a wide variety of food—great wings, sandwiches, salads, etc... kids meals are inexpensive and come with a drink and a side... **"**

Children's menu......................✓	$$$..Prices
Changing station ....✓	❸ ....Customer service
Highchairs/boosters..................✓	❸ ....Stroller access

WWW.QUAKERSTEAKANDLUBE.COM

VALLEY VIEW—5935 CANAL RD (OFF ROCKSIDE RD); 216.986.9500; SU-TH
11-12, F-SA 11-1

Red Robin

"...*very kid-oriented—loud, balloons, bright lights, colorful decor and a cheerful staff make Red Robin a favorite among parents and children... the food is mainly burgers (beef or chicken)... loud music covers even the most boisterous of screaming... lots of kids—all the time... sometimes the wait can be long, but the arcade games and balloons help pass the time...* **"**

Children's menu	✓	$$	Prices
Changing station	✓	❹	Customer service
Highchairs/boosters	✓	❹	Stroller access

WWW.REDROBIN.COM

INDEPENDENCE—6750 ROCKSIDE RD (AT BRECKSVILLE RD); 216.642.0881;
SU-TH 11-10, F-SA 11-11

ORANGE VILLAGE—7009 ORANGE PL (AT CHAGRIN BLVD); 216.378.9362;
SU-TH 11-10, F-SA 11-11

Ruby Tuesday

"...*nice variety of healthy choices on the kids' menu—turkey, spaghetti, chicken tenders... you can definitely find something healthy here... prices are on the high side, but at least everyone can find something they like... service is fast and efficient... my daughter makes a mess and they never let me clean it up... your typical chain, but it works—you'll be happy to see ample aisle space, storage for your stroller, and attentive staff...* **"**

Children's menu	✓	$$	Prices
Changing station	✓	❹	Customer service
Highchairs/boosters	✓	❸	Stroller access

WWW.RUBYTUESDAY.COM

BEACHWOOD—24325 CHAGRIN BLVD (AT RICHMOND RD); 216.464.2700;
SU-TH 11-11, F-SA 11-12; PARKING IN FRONT OF BLDG

RICHMOND HEIGHTS—691 RICHMOND RD (AT RICHMOND MALL);
440.442.8877; SU-TH 11-11, F-SA 11-12; PARKING IN FRONT OF BLDG

Timberfire

"...*great casual food... restaurant looks like a log house... when you want to get away from the chain restaurants, try this one for the kids... food that's yummy for parents (steaks, chops) and little ones (pizza)... a nice outdoor patio for nice weather...* **"**

Children's menu	✓	$$$	Prices
Changing station	✓	❸	Customer service
Highchairs/boosters	✓	❸	Stroller access

WWW.TIMBERFIRE.COM

CHAGRIN FALLS—8258 E WASHINGTON ST (AT CHILLICOTHE RD);
440.708.2222; M-TH 5-9, F 5-11, SA 4-11, SU 11-8

Tommy's

"...*specialize in vegetarian dishes with a truly unique and extensive menu... packed during weekday lunches with parents and strollers... sometimes service can be slow, but it's OK to have an impatient little one in this friendly atmosphere...very laid-back feel to the entire place...* **"**

Children's menu	✗	$$$	Prices
Changing station	✗	❸	Customer service
Highchairs/boosters	✓	❸	Stroller access

WWW.TOMMYSCOVENTRY.COM

restaurants

CLEVELAND HEIGHTS—1824 COVENTRY RD (AT LANCASHIRE RD);
216.321.7757; M-TH 7:30-10, F-SA 7:30-11, SU 9-10

Yours Truly Restaurant ★★★★★

"...*a very nice place for family dining... it's easy to fit strollers, highchairs, child seats, etc... good burgers, fries and other grilled items... one of my family's favorite places to eat... good, basic comfort food—an easy night out...* **"**

Children's menu .... ✓ $$ .... Prices
Changing station .... ✓   ❹ .... Customer service
Highchairs/boosters .... ✓   ❹ .... Stroller access

WWW.YTR.COM

BEACHWOOD—25300 CHAGRIN BLVD (AT RICHMOND RD); 216.464.4848; M-SA 6:30-11, SU 7:30-9; PARKING LOT

CHAGRIN FALLS—30 N MAIN ST (AT PLAZA DR); 440.247.3232; M-SA 6:30-11, SU 7:30-9; PARKING BEHIND BLDG

GATES MILLS—6675 WILSON MILLS RD (AT SOM CTR RD); 440.461.0000; M-SA 6:30-11, SU 7:30-9

participate in our survey at

Suburbs – West Side

★★★★★
"lila picks"

- ★ Bearden's Restaurant
- ★ Buca Di Beppo
- ★ Nuevo Acapulco Mexican Restaurant
- ★ Ruby Tuesday

Bearden's Restaurant　★★★★★

"...a fun place to take kids of all ages... bare bones decor... has a family-friendly feel... the train that rides along the ceiling wall is very entertaining for little ones... not the most healthy dinner, but the burgers are great...**"**

Children's menu	✓	$$	Prices
Changing station	✗	❹	Customer service
Highchairs/boosters	✓	❹	Stroller access

WWW.BEARDENS-CLEVELAND.COM

ROCKY RIVER—19985 LAKE RD (AT CORNWALL RD); 440.331.7850; M-TH 11-8:30, F-SA 11-9

Beef O'Brady's　★★★⯨☆

"...good place for a quick bite and a beer... the best wings around... dim lighting and layout can make it tricky to navigate a stroller... the O'Bradys burger is great... family-friendly atmosphere—kids can play and have a good time without disturbing other patrons...**"**

Children's menu	✓	$$	Prices
Changing station	✓	❹	Customer service
Highchairs/boosters	✓	❹	Stroller access

WWW.BEEFOBRADYS.COM

STRONGSVILLE—17692 PEARL RD (AT DRAKE RD); 440.572.4466; M-SA 11-11, SU 12-10

Buca di Beppo　★★★★★

"...massive Italian portions make this a great deal of a meal... entertaining atmosphere and attitiude... typically loud so crying little ones won't even be heard... be sure to share the meals and be ready for a doggy bag...**"**

Children's menu	✗	$$$	Prices
Changing station	✗	❹	Customer service
Highchairs/boosters	✓	❸	Stroller access

WWW.BUCADIBEPPO.COM

STRONGSVILLE—16677 SOUTH PARK CTR (AT HOWE RD); 440.846.6262; M-TH 5-10, F 5-11, SA 12-11, SU 12-9

WESTLAKE—23575 DETROIT RD (AT CLAGUE RD); 440.356.2276; M-TH 5-10, F 5-11, SA 3-11, SU 12-9

Cheesecake Factory, The ★★★★☆

"...although their cheesecake is good, we come here for the kid-friendly atmosphere and selection of good food... eclectic menu has something for everyone... they will bring your tot a plate of yogurt, cheese, bananas and bread free of charge... we love how flexible they are—they'll make whatever my kids want... lots of mommies here... always fun and always crazy... no real kids menu, but the pizza is great to share... waits can be really long... **"**

Children's menu	✗	$$$	Prices
Changing station	✓	❹	Customer service
Highchairs/boosters	✓	❸	Stroller access

WWW.THECHEESECAKEFACTORY.COM

WESTLAKE—148 CROCKER PARK BLVD (AT CROCKER PARK MALL); 440.808.1818; M-TH 11:30-11, F-SA 11:30-12:30, SU 10-11; MALL PARKING

Chili's Grill & Bar ★★★½☆

"...family-friendly, mild Mexican fare... delicious ribs, soups, salads... kids' menu and crayons as you sit down... on the noisy side, so you don't mind if your kids talk in their usual loud voices... service is excellent... fun night out with the family... a wide variety of menu selections for kids and their parents—all at a reasonable price... best chicken fingers on any kids' menu... **"**

Children's menu	✓	$$	Prices
Changing station	✓	❹	Customer service
Highchairs/boosters	✓	❹	Stroller access

WWW.CHILIS.COM

NORTH OLMSTED—25061 COUNTRY CLUB RD (OFF RT 480); 440.777.0117; SU-TH 11-11, F-SA 11-12

Cici's Pizza ★★★★☆

"...a great buffet for easy dining with kids... pizza at the right price... kids 3 and under eat free... very crowded during lunch and dinner rushes... not much room for strollers, but they'll help you find a place to stash it... they always have birthday parties and it's usually very crowded and noisy... pizza, pasta and salad buffet for under $10... **"**

Children's menu	✓	$	Prices
Changing station	✓	❹	Customer service
Highchairs/boosters	✓	❹	Stroller access

WWW.CICISPIZZA.COM

BROOKLYN—4824 RIDGE RD (AT DELORA AVE); 216.661.3870; SU-TH 11-10, F-SA 11-11

Dave & Buster's ★★★☆☆

"...lively bar and dining room paired with an adult style arcade... games and television throughout the restaurant give you plenty to keep your eyes on... decent food... can get a little loud and smoky for your average tot... most games are geared for adults... keep your eyes on your kids—it gets crowded... **"**

Children's menu	✓	$$$	Prices
Changing station	✓	❹	Customer service
Highchairs/boosters	✓	❹	Stroller access

WWW.DAVEANDBUSTERS.COM

WESTLAKE—25735 1ST ST (AT COLUMBIA RD); 440.892.1415; SU-W 11:30-12, TH 11:30-1, F-SA 11:30-2

Don Pablo's ★★★★☆

"...yummy Mexican dishes... spacious and super kid-friendly—we've been coming here since our baby was 2 weeks old... kid's meals are inexpensive and plentiful... my son loves playing with the dough and

participate in our survey at

the meal arrives in no time... fun, boisterous setting... can get busy, but you generally get a table with little delay... **"**

Children's menu ....✓ $$ .... Prices
Changing station.....................✓   ❹ .... Customer service
Highchairs/boosters ....✓   ❹ ....Stroller access

WWW.DONPABLOS.COM

BROOKLYN—10310 CASCADE CROSSING (AT TIEDEMAN RD); 216.265.8284; SU-TH 11-10, F-SA 11-11

Golden Sea Chinese Restaurant

Children's menu ....✗   ✗ ....Changing station
Highchairs/boosters ....✓

PARMA—5270 PEARL RD (AT BROOKPARK RD); 216.661.5990; SU-TH 11-10, F-SA 11-11

Harpo's Sports Café   ★★★⯪☆

"...*three-level sports bar is part tailgate, part family restaurant, and thoroughly enjoyable... the smoke-free game room on the upper level offers air hockey, foozball, and video games—and is kid-friendly...* **"**

Children's menu ....✓ $$$ .... Prices
Changing station.....................✓   ❸ .... Customer service
Highchairs/boosters ....✓   ❸ ....Stroller access

WWW.GOHARPOS.COM

BROOK PARK—5777 SMITH RD (AT SNOW RD); 216.267.7777; M-F 11-2AM, SA-SU 3-2AM

STRONGSVILLE—19654 W 130TH ST (OFF BOSTON RD); 440.846.7777; M-F 11-2AM, SA-SU 3-2AM

Johnny Rockets   ★★★★☆

"...*burgers, fries and a shake served up in a 50's style diner... we love the singing waiters—they're always good for a giggle... my daughter is enthralled with the juke box and straw dispenser... sit at the counter and watch the cooks prepare the food... simple, satisfying and always a hit with the little ones...* **"**

Children's menu ....✓ $$ .... Prices
Changing station.....................✗   ❹ .... Customer service
Highchairs/boosters ....✓   ❸ ....Stroller access

WWW.JOHNNYROCKETS.COM

STRONGSVILLE—272 SOUTHPARK CTR (AT HOWE RD); 440.878.9040; M-TH 11-11, F-SA 11-2AM; STREET PARKING

Longhorn Steakhouse   ★★★★☆

"...*for meat and seafood lovers... the staff totally gets 'the kid thing' here... they bring out snacks, get the orders going quickly, and frequently check back for things like new spoons and napkins... lots of things for baby to look at... get there early or call ahead to avoid the wait...* **"**

Children's menu ....✓ $$$ .... Prices
Changing station.....................✓   ❹ .... Customer service
Highchairs/boosters ....✓   ❸ ....Stroller access

WWW.LONGHORNSTEAKHOUSE.COM

FAIRVIEW PARK—20999 CENTER RIDGE RD (AT WESTGATE MALL); 440.356.5433; SU-TH 11-10, F-SA 11-11

STRONGSVILLE—17211 SOUTH PARK CTR (AT HOWE RD); 440.238.7917; SU-TH 11-10, F-SA 11-11

restaurants

Max's Deli

"...located in the heart of downtown Rocky River... always some of the best sandwiches and desserts in the area... lots of little ones make it a great place to meet for lunch with fellow parents... kids can drool over the dessert case... **"**

Children's menu.......................... ✓ $$$..Prices
Changing station .... ✗   ❸ ....Customer service
Highchairs/boosters...................... ✓   ❸ ....Stroller access

ROCKY RIVER—19337 DETROIT RD (AT WRIGHT AVE); 440.356.2226; M-TH
 11-11, F-SA 11-12, SU 10-9; PARKING LOT

Moosehead Saloon

"...laid back bar atmosphere on the border of westlake and bay village... great food and down-to-earth service...delicious bar food... **"**

Children's menu.......................... ✓ $$$..Prices
Changing station .... ✓   ❸ ....Customer service
Highchairs/boosters...................... ✓   ❸ ....Stroller access

WESTLAKE—694 DOVER CTR RD (AT 2ND ST); 440.871.7742; M-TH 11:30-11,
 F-SA 11:30-12, SU 12-10

Nuevo Acapulco Mexican Restaurant

"...the best Mexican food in town... reasonable prices... if you love Mexican, you will love this place... casual and kid-friendly... fast service... enormous portions are great for sharing... the friendly staff and colorful decor have made this a favorite of our son ... busy on Friday and Saturday nights... **"**

Children's menu.......................... ✓ $$..Prices
Changing station .... ✗   ❹ ....Customer service
Highchairs/boosters...................... ✓   ❸ ....Stroller access

WWW.NUEVOACAPULCO.COM

BEREA—804 FRONT ST (AT SHELDON RD); 440.234.2500; M-TH 11-10, F-SA
 11-11, SU 12-10

NORTH OLMSTED—24409 LORAIN RD (AT WALTER RD); 440.734.3100; M-TH
 11-10, F-SA 11-11, SU 12-10

Red Robin

"...very kid-oriented—loud, balloons, bright lights, colorful decor and a cheerful staff make Red Robin a favorite among parents and children... the food is mainly burgers (beef or chicken)... loud music covers even the most boisterous of screaming... lots of kids—all the time... sometimes the wait can be long, but the arcade games and balloons help pass the time... **"**

Children's menu.......................... ✓ $$..Prices
Changing station .... ✓   ❹ ....Customer service
Highchairs/boosters...................... ✓   ❹ ....Stroller access

WWW.REDROBIN.COM

NORTH OLMSTED—4949 GREAT NORTHERN BLVD (AT BROOKPARK RD);
 440.734.6070; SU-TH 11-10, F-SA 11-11

Rocky River Brewing Company

"...great indoor atmosphere plus a nice outdoor patio in the heart of downtown family-friendly Rocky River... young crowd makes it welcoming to little ones... nice bar and micro brews help you deal with any crying kid... also have a delicious Sunday brunch... **"**

Children's menu.......................... ✓ $$$..Prices
Changing station .... ✓   ❸ ....Customer service
Highchairs/boosters...................... ✓   ❸ ....Stroller access

ROCKY RIVER—21290 CTR RDG RD (AT WAGAR RD); 440.895.2739; M-W
11:30-11, TH-SA 11:30-1, SU 11-11

Romano's Macaroni Grill ★★★★☆

❝...*family oriented and tasty... noisy so nobody cares if your kids make noise... the staff goes out of their way to make families feel welcome... they even provide slings by the table for infant carriers... the noise level is pretty constant so it's not too loud, but loud enough so that crying babies don't disturb the other patrons... good kids' menu with somewhat healthy items... crayons for kids to color on the paper tablecloths...* **❞**

Children's menu	✓	$$$	Prices
Changing station	✓	❹	Customer service
Highchairs/boosters	✓	❹	Stroller access

WWW.MACARONIGRILL.COM

NORTH OLMSTED—25001 COUNTRY CLUB BLVD (OFF RT 252);
440.734.9980; SU-TH 11-10, F-SA 11-11

STRONGSVILLE—17095 SOUTH PARK CTR (AT ROYALTON RD);
440.878.3000; SU-TH 11-10, F-SA 11-11

Ruby Tuesday ★★★★★

❝...*nice variety of healthy choices on the kids' menu—turkey, spaghetti, chicken tenders... you can definitely find something healthy here... prices are on the high side, but at least everyone can find something they like... service is fast and efficient... my daughter makes a mess and they never let me clean it up... your typical chain, but it works—you'll be happy to see ample aisle space, storage for your stroller, and attentive staff...* **❞**

Children's menu	✓	$$	Prices
Changing station	✓	❹	Customer service
Highchairs/boosters	✓	❸	Stroller access

WWW.RUBYTUESDAY.COM

NORTH OLMSTED—26774 LORAIN RD (AT DOVER CTR RD); 440.716.9499;
SU-TH 11-11, F-SA 11-12; PARKING IN FRONT OF BLDG

SEVEN HILLS—7331 BROADVIEW RD (AT W PLEASANT VALLEY RD);
216.447.1662; SU-TH 11-11, F-SA 11-12; PARKING IN FRONT OF BLDG

restaurants

Lake & Geauga

★ ★ ★ ★ ★

"lila picks"

★ Yours Truly Restaurant

Bravo Cucina Italiana ★★★★⯪

"...good food, decent prices and family friendly... we like it because it isn't a 'kids' restaurant—it definitely caters primarily to adults, but they are great with kids... my son is always welcomed there with balloons and lots of attention... great kids menu and friendly staff... **"**

Children's menu	✓	$$$	Prices
Changing station	✓	❹	Customer service
Highchairs/boosters	✓	❹	Stroller access

WWW.BRAVOITALIAN.COM

MENTOR—7787 REYNOLDS RD; 440.946.2090; SU-TH 11-10, F-SA 11-11

Don Pablo's ★★★★☆

"...yummy Mexican dishes... spacious and super kid-friendly—we've been coming here since our baby was 2 weeks old... kid's meals are inexpensive and plentiful... my son loves playing with the dough and the meal arrives in no time... fun, boisterous setting... can get busy, but you generally get a table with little delay... **"**

Children's menu	✓	$$	Prices
Changing station	✓	❹	Customer service
Highchairs/boosters	✓	❹	Stroller access

WWW.DONPABLOS.COM

WILLOUGHBY—36455 EUCLID AVE (OFF RT 91); 440.954.3541; SU-TH 11-10, F-SA 11-11

Johnny Mango ★★★★★

"...smokefree unique ambience with yummy food and drinks, including a juice bar... truly a 'world café'... every month has a new theme.. Open for lunch and dinner, brunch on weekends... kids are certainly welcome and mine loves the quesadillas... **"**

Children's menu	✗	$$	Prices
Changing station	✗	❺	Customer service
Highchairs/boosters	✗	❹	Stroller access

WWW.JMANGO.COM

WILLOUGHBY—4113 ERIE ST (AT 2ND ST); 440.975.8811; M-TH 11-10, F 11-11, SA 9-11, SU 9-10

Longhorn Steakhouse ★★★★☆

"...for meat and seafood lovers... the staff totally gets 'the kid thing' here... they bring out snacks, get the orders going quickly, and frequently check back for things like new spoons and napkins... lots of things for baby to look at... get there early or call ahead to avoid the wait... **"**

Children's menu	✓	$$$	Prices

participate in our survey at

| Changing station | ✓ | ❹ | Customer service |
| Highchairs/boosters | ✓ | ❸ | Stroller access |

WWW.LONGHORNSTEAKHOUSE.COM

MENTOR—9557 MENTOR AVE (AT OLD JOHNNYCAKE); 440.639.5103; SU-TH 11-10, F-SA 11-11

Red Robin ★★★⯪☆

"...very kid-oriented—loud, balloons, bright lights, colorful decor and a cheerful staff make Red Robin a favorite among parents and children... the food is mainly burgers (beef or chicken)... loud music covers even the most boisterous of screaming... lots of kids—all the time... sometimes the wait can be long, but the arcade games and balloons help pass the time... **"**

Children's menu	✓	$$	Prices
Changing station	✓	❹	Customer service
Highchairs/boosters	✓	❹	Stroller access

WWW.REDROBIN.COM

WILLOUGHBY—36565 EUCLID AVE (AT NORTHRIDGE DR); 440.602.9766; SU-TH 11-10, F-SA 11-11

Smokey Bones BBQ ★★★★☆

"...reasonably healthy food for kids—not fried chicken fingers and fries... lots of TVs to entertain kids so adults can have a little time to talk... volume control at each table, stations often set to Nickelodeon... unique holders for car seats that cradle the seats... **"**

Children's menu	✓	$$$	Prices
Changing station	✓	❹	Customer service
Highchairs/boosters	✓	❹	Stroller access

WWW.SMOKEYBONES.COM

MENTOR—7725 REYNOLDS RD (OFF LAKELAND PKY); 440.942.0993; SU-TH 11-10, F-SA 11-11

Yours Truly Restaurant ★★★★★

"...a very nice place for family dining... it's easy to fit strollers, highchairs, child seats, etc... good burgers, fries and other grilled items... one of my family's favorite places to eat... good, basic comfort food—an easy night out... **"**

Children's menu	✓	$$	Prices
Changing station	✓	❹	Customer service
Highchairs/boosters	✓	❹	Stroller access

WWW.YTR.COM

MENTOR—7274 CENTER ST (AT NOWLEN ST); 440.255.3003; M-SA 6:30-11, SU 7:30-9; PARKING LOT

Lorain & Medina

★★★★★

"lila picks"

★ Ruby Tuesday

★ Yours Truly Restaurant

Cici's Pizza
★★★★☆

"...a great buffet for easy dining with kids... pizza at the right price... kids 3 and under eat free... very crowded during lunch and dinner rushes... not much room for strollers, but they'll help you find a place to stash it... they always have birthday parties and it's usually very crowded and noisy... pizza, pasta and salad buffet for under $10..."

Children's menu...................... ✓ | $ ....Prices
Changing station .... ✓ | ❹ ....Customer service
Highchairs/boosters.................... ✓ | ❹ .... Stroller access

WWW.CICISPIZZA.COM

AVON—36050-E DETROIT RD (AT CENTER RD); 440.934.3855; SU-TH 11-10, F-SA 11-11

BRUNSWICK—3362 CENTER RD (AT CARPENTER RD); 330.225.8128; SU-TH 11-10, F-SA 11-11

LORAIN—1980 COOPER FOSTER PARK RD (AT AMHERST PLAZA); 440.282.1640; SU-TH 11-10, F-SA 11-11

Fazoli's
★★★½☆

"...quick, easy and satisfying Italian food... spacious and comfortable... free breadsticks to keep little minds in check before the meatballs and pasta arrive... a nice step up from the easy fast-food trap... service is quick and the food is good..."

Children's menu...................... ✓ | $$...Prices
Changing station .... ✓ | ❹ ....Customer service
Highchairs/boosters.................... ✓ | ❸ .... Stroller access

WWW.FAZOLIS.COM

ELYRIA—1540 W RIVER RD N (AT MIDWAY MALL); 440.324.1300; SU-TH 10:30-10, F-SA 10:30-11

Longhorn Steakhouse
★★★★☆

"...for meat and seafood lovers... the staff totally gets 'the kid thing' here... they bring out snacks, get the orders going quickly, and frequently check back for things like new spoons and napkins... lots of things for baby to look at... get there early or call ahead to avoid the wait..."

Children's menu...................... ✓ | $$$......................................Prices
Changing station .... ✓ | ❹ ....Customer service
Highchairs/boosters.................... ✓ | ❸ .... Stroller access

WWW.LONGHORNSTEAKHOUSE.COM

MEDINA—4907 GRANDE BLVD (AT FENN RD); 330.721.4585; SU-TH 11-10, F-SA 11-11

participate in our survey at

Quaker Steak and Lube

"...a great place to bring the kids... a wide variety of food—great wings, sandwiches, salads, etc... kids meals are inexpensive and come with a drink and a side...**"**

Children's menu ....✓ $$$ .... Prices
Changing station.......................✓   **❸** .... Customer service
Highchairs/boosters ....✓   **❸** ....Stroller access

WWW.QUAKERSTEAKANDLUBE.COM

SHEFFIELD VILLAGE—4900 TRANSPORTATION DR (OFF RT 254); 440.934.2378; M-W 11-12, TH-SA 11-2, SU 11-11

Red Robin

"...very kid-oriented—loud, balloons, bright lights, colorful decor and a cheerful staff make Red Robin a favorite among parents and children... the food is mainly burgers (beef or chicken)... loud music covers even the most boisterous of screaming... lots of kids—all the time... sometimes the wait can be long, but the arcade games and balloons help pass the time...**"**

Children's menu ....✓ $$ .... Prices
Changing station.......................✓   **❹** .... Customer service
Highchairs/boosters ....✓   **❹** ....Stroller access

WWW.REDROBIN.COM

AVON—35858 DETROIT AVE (AT DETROIT RD); 440.937.0260; SU-TH 11-10, F-SA 11-11

Ruby Tuesday

"...nice variety of healthy choices on the kids' menu—turkey, spaghetti, chicken tenders... you can definitely find something healthy here... prices are on the high side, but at least everyone can find something they like... service is fast and efficient... my daughter makes a mess and they never let me clean it up... your typical chain, but it works—you'll be happy to see ample aisle space, storage for your stroller, and attentive staff...**"**

Children's menu ....✓ $$ .... Prices
Changing station.......................✓   **❹** .... Customer service
Highchairs/boosters ....✓   **❸** ....Stroller access

WWW.RUBYTUESDAY.COM

ELYRIA—5274 ABBE RD N (AT DETROIT RD); 440.934.1200; SU-TH 11-11, F-SA 11-12; PARKING IN FRONT OF BLDG

MEDINA—1001 N COURT ST (AT REAGAN PKY); 330.723.6206; SU-TH 11-11, F-SA 11-12; PARKING IN FRONT OF BLDG

Sorrento's Ristorante Italiano

Children's menu ....✓   ✗ ....Changing station
Highchairs/boosters ....✓

ELYRIA—108 ANTIOCH DR (AT LORRAIN COUNTY COMMUNITY COLLEGE); 440.366.6620; M-SA 11-10, SU 4-10

Yours Truly Restaurant

"...a very nice place for family dining... it's easy to fit strollers, highchairs, child seats, etc... good burgers, fries and other grilled items... one of my family's favorite places to eat... good, basic comfort food—an easy night out...**"**

Children's menu ....✓ $$ .... Prices
Changing station.......................✓   **❹** .... Customer service
Highchairs/boosters ....✓   **❹** ....Stroller access

WWW.YTR.COM

MEDINA—3725 MEDINA RD (AT VICTOR DR); 330.722.5800; M-SA 6:30AM-11PM, SU 7:30AM-9PM

Portage & Summit

★★★★★
"lila picks"

★ Ruby Tuesday
★ Yours Truly Restaurant

Chili's Grill & Bar ★★★½☆

❝...family-friendly, mild Mexican fare... delicious ribs, soups, salads... kids' menu and crayons as you sit down... on the noisy side, so you don't mind if your kids talk in their usual loud voices... service is excellent... fun night out with the family... a wide variety of menu selections for kids and their parents—all at a reasonable price... best chicken fingers on any kids' menu... ❞

Children's menu	✓	$$	Prices
Changing station	✓	❹	Customer service
Highchairs/boosters	✓	❹	Stroller access

WWW.CHILIS.COM

AKRON—4022 MEDINA RD (AT SPRINGSIDE DR); 330.668.2882; SU-TH 11-11, F-SA 11-12

Cici's Pizza ★★★★☆

❝...a great buffet for easy dining with kids... pizza at the right price... kids 3 and under eat free... very crowded during lunch and dinner rushes... not much room for strollers, but they'll help you find a place to stash it... they always have birthday parties and it's usually very crowded and noisy... pizza, pasta and salad buffet for under $10... ❞

Children's menu	✓	$	Prices
Changing station	✓	❹	Customer service
Highchairs/boosters	✓	❹	Stroller access

WWW.CICISPIZZA.COM

STREETSBORO—1276 STATE RT 303 (AT CLEVELAND CANTON RD); 330.422.1760; SU-TH 11-10, F-SA 11-11

Don Pablo's ★★★★☆

❝...yummy Mexican dishes... spacious and super kid-friendly—we've been coming here since our baby was 2 weeks old... kid's meals are inexpensive and plentiful... my son loves playing with the dough and the meal arrives in no time... fun, boisterous setting... can get busy, but you generally get a table with little delay... ❞

Children's menu	✓	$$	Prices
Changing station	✓	❹	Customer service
Highchairs/boosters	✓	❹	Stroller access

WWW.DONPABLOS.COM

AKRON—145 MONTROSE W AVE (AT RT 21); 330.666.0239; SU-TH 11-10, F-SA 11-11

participate in our survey at

Longhorn Steakhouse

"...for meat and seafood lovers... the staff totally gets 'the kid thing' here... they bring out snacks, get the orders going quickly, and frequently check back for things like new spoons and napkins... lots of things for baby to look at... get there early or call ahead to avoid the wait... **"**

Children's menu ....✓ $$$ .... Prices
Changing station.......................✓   ❹ .... Customer service
Highchairs/boosters ....✓   ❸ ....Stroller access

WWW.LONGHORNSTEAKHOUSE.COM

CUYAHOGA FALLS—443 HOWE AVE (OFF MAIN ST); 330.922.3391; SU-TH 11-10, F-3A 11-11

Romano's Macaroni Grill

"...family oriented and tasty... noisy so nobody cares if your kids make noise... the staff goes out of their way to make families feel welcome... they even provide slings by the table for infant carriers... the noise level is pretty constant so it's not too loud, but loud enough so that crying babies don't disturb the other patrons... good kids' menu with somewhat healthy items... crayons for kids to color on the paper tablecloths... **"**

Children's menu ....✓ $$$ .... Prices
Changing station.......................✓   ❹ .... Customer service
Highchairs/boosters ....✓   ❹ ....Stroller access

WWW.MACARONIGRILL.COM

AKRON—41 SPRINGSIDE DR (OFF MEDINA RD); 330.665.3881; SU-TH 11-10, F-SA 11-11

Ruby Tuesday

"...nice variety of healthy choices on the kids' menu—turkey, spaghetti, chicken tenders... you can definitely find something healthy here... prices are on the high side, but at least everyone can find something they like... service is fast and efficient... my daughter makes a mess and they never let me clean it up... your typical chain, but it works—you'll be happy to see ample aisle space, storage for your stroller, and attentive staff... **"**

Children's menu ....✓ $$ .... Prices
Changing station.......................✓   ❹ .... Customer service
Highchairs/boosters ....✓   ❸ ....Stroller access

WWW.RUBYTUESDAY.COM

AKRON—3265 W MARKET ST (AT SUMMIT MALL); 330.869.5990; SU-TH 11-11, F-SA 11-12; PARKING IN FRONT OF BLDG

AURORA—7135 N AURORA RD (AT PETTIBONE RD); 330.995.0401; SU-TH 11-11, F-SA 11-12; PARKING IN FRONT OF BLDG

STREETSBORO—9687 STATE RT 14 (AT SUMMIT MALL); 330.626.5115; SU-TH 11-11, F-SA 11-12; PARKING IN FRONT OF BLDG

Spaghetti Warehouse

"...lots of Italian choices... we never go wrong with their delicious pasta... large portions, so I can get away with ordering one dish and sharing it with my tot... they have a kids-eat-free night, which is great with multiple kids... prices are reasonable... **"**

Children's menu ....✓ $$ .... Prices
Changing station.......................✓   ❹ .... Customer service
Highchairs/boosters ....✓   ❹ ....Stroller access

WWW.MEATBALLS.COM

AKRON—510 S MAIN ST (OFF RT 261); 330.374.0025; SU-TH 11-10, F-SA 11-11

Yours Truly Restaurant

"...*a very nice place for family dining... it's easy to fit strollers, highchairs, child seats, etc... good burgers, fries and other grilled items... one of my family's favorite places to eat... good, basic comfort food—an easy night out...* **"**

Children's menu........................... ✓ $$... Prices
Changing station .... ✓ ❹ ....Customer service
Highchairs/boosters..................... ✓ ❹ .... Stroller access

WWW.YTR.COM

HUDSON—36 S MAIN ST (AT RAVENNA ST); 330.656.2900; M-SA 6:30-11, SU
  7:30-10; PARKING LOT

doulas & lactation consultants

Editor's Note: Doulas and lactation consultants provide a wide range of services and are very difficult to classify, let alone rate. In fact the terms 'doula' and 'lactation consultant' have very specific industry definitions that are far more complex than we are able to cover in this brief guide. For this reason we have decided to list only those businesses and individuals who received overwhelmingly positive reviews, without listing the reviewers' comments.

Greater Cleveland Area

Association of Labor Assistants & Childbirth Educators (ALACE)

Labor doula .... ✓   ✗ .... Postpartum doula
Pre & post natal massage .... ✗   ✗ .... Lactation consultant

WWW.ALACE.ORG

CLEVELAND—617.441.2500

Doulas of North America (DONA)

Labor doula .... ✓   ✓ .... Postpartum doula
Pre & post natal massage .... ✗   ✗ .... Lactation consultant

WWW.DONA.ORG

CLEVELAND—888.788.3662

La Leche League

Labor doula .... ✗   ✗ .... Postpartum doula
Pre & post natal massage .... ✗   ✓ .... Lactation consultant

WWW.LALECHELEAGUE.ORG

CLEVELAND—VARIOUS LOCATIONS; 847.519.7730; CHECK SCHEDULE
  ONLINE

UHHS Chagrin Highlands Medical Center (Lactation Center)

Labor doula .... ✗   ✗ .... Postpartum doula
Pre & post natal massage .... ✗   ✓ .... Lactation consultant

WWW.MACDONALDWOMENSHOSPITAL.ORG

ORANGE VILLAGE—3909 ORANGE PL (AT HARVARD RD); 216.595.5353; CALL
  FOR SCHEDULE

UHHS Westlake Medical Center (Lactation Center)

Labor doula .... ✗   ✗ .... Postpartum doula
Pre & post natal massage .... ✗   ✓ .... Lactation consultant

WWW.UHHS.COM

WESTLAKE—960 CLAGUE RD (AT DETROIT RD); 440.250.2035; CALL FOR
  SCHEDULE

participate in our survey at

exercise

City of Cleveland

★★★★★

"lila picks"

★ Stroller Fit

One To One Fitness Center ★★★★☆

"...for about $35 a month, you can join one of the nicest, cleanest gyms in the area... and they have free daycare for babies 12 weeks and older..."

Prenatal	✗	$	Prices
Mommy & me	✗	❺	Decor
Child care available	✓	❸	Customer service

WWW.CASE.EDU/FINADMIN/SECURITY/121/121.HTM

CLEVELAND—2130 ADELBERT RD (AT UNIVERSITY HOSPITALS OF CLEVELAND); 216.368.1120; CHECK SCHEDULE ONLINE

Parma Community General Hospital (Health Education Center) ★★★★☆

"...great variety of exercise classes and excellent instructors... great for mental, emotional, and physical health... whether it's aerobics, self defense for children and adults, golf, yoga, parent/toddler gym, crafts or stress management, there's something for everyone in the family..."

Prenatal	✗	$$$$	Prices
Mommy & me	✗	❺	Decor
Child care available	✗	❸	Customer service

WWW.PARMAHOSPITAL.ORG

CLEVELAND—7007 POWERS BLVD (AT RIDGE RD); 440.743.4030; CALL FOR SCHEDULE

Stroller Fit ★★★★★

"...a great workout for parents and the kids are entertained the whole time... a great way to ease back into exercise after your baby's birth... the instructor is knowledgeable about fitness and keeping babies happy... motivating, supportive, and fun for kids and moms... sometimes they even set up a play group for after class... not just a good workout, but also a great chance to meet other moms and kids..."

Prenatal	✗	$$$	Prices
Mommy & me	✓	❸	Decor
Child care available	✗	❸	Customer service

WWW.STROLLERFIT.COM

CLEVELAND—VARIOUS LOCATIONS; 440.238.0581

YMCA ★★★★☆

"...the variety of fitness programs offered is astounding... class types and quality vary from facility to facility, but it's a must for new moms to

participate in our survey at

check out... most facilities offer some kind of kids' activities or childcare so you can time your workouts around the classes... aerobics, yoga, pool—our Y even offers Pilates now... my favorite classes are the mom & baby yoga... the best bang for your buck... they have it all—great programs that meet the needs of a diverse range of families... **"**

Prenatal	✓	$$$	Prices
Mommy & me	✓	❸	Decor
Child care available	✓	❸	Customer service

WWW.YMCA.COM

CLEVELAND—15501 LORAIN AVE; 440.871.6885; CHECK SCHEDULE ONLINE

CLEVELAND—??00 PROSPECT AVE; 440.871.6885; CHECK SCHEDULE ONLINE

exercise

Suburbs – East Side

★★★★★
"lila picks"

★ Pilates For Moms

Atma Center ★★★★☆

"...the prenatal, postnatal and mommy and me yoga classes are excellent... the prenatal yoga could have easily replaced Lamaze in my experience!..."

Prenatal	✗	$$$	Prices
Mommy & me	✗	❹	Decor
Child care available	✗	❹	Customer service

WWW.ATMACENTER.COM

CLEVELAND HEIGHTS—2319 LEE RD (AT DELLWOOD RD); 216.371.9760; M-TH 10-8, F-SA 10-6, SU 10-4

Cleveland Heights Community Center ★★★★☆

"...prenatal pilates class offered is excellent... the class kept me feeling good for the entire 9 months... the ice rink is great for older kids... they provide lessons too!..."

Prenatal	✓	$$	Prices
Mommy & me	✓	❸	Decor
Child care available	✗	❸	Customer service

WWW.CLEVELANDHEIGHTS.COM/ARTSREC_PARKS.ASP

CLEVELAND HEIGHTS—1 MONTICELLO BLVD (AT MAYFIELD RD); 216.691.7373; CHECK SCHEDULE ONLINE; PARKING LOT

Evolution Yoga Studio ★★★★☆

"...great prenatal class... wonderful techniques that really helped strengthen my body... I also love the mommy and me classes... they make it so much fun..."

Prenatal	✓	$$$	Prices
Mommy & me	✓	❺	Decor
Child care available	✗	❸	Customer service

WWW.EVOLUTIONYOGASTUDIO.COM

BEACHWOOD—3737 PARK EAST DR (AT CHAGRIN BLVD); 216.595.9642; CHECK SCHEDULE ONLINE; PARKING LOT

Pilates for Moms ★★★★★

"...a great pre- or postnatal class... really helps you to learn ways to improve your posture and avoid the aches and pains related to pregnancy... relaxing and essential for my well-being... these classes totally helped me get back into shape after my baby was born... the instructor is extremely knowledgeable, friendly and fun..."

Prenatal	✓	$$$	Prices
Mommy & me	✗	❹	Decor

Child care available...................... ✗   **❺**........................ Customer service

WWW.PILATESMOM.COM

CLEVELAND HEIGHTS—1700 CREST RD (AT WOOD RD); 440.840.6379; CLASS
  SCHEDULES ONLINE

UHHS Chagrin Highlands Medical Center

Prenatal...................................... ✓   ✓............................ Mommy & me

Child care available...................... ✗

WWW.MACDONALDWOMENSHOSPITAL.ORG

ORANGE VILLAGE—3909 ORANGE PL (AT HARVARD RD); 216.844.4000; CALL
  FOR SCHEDULE

Suburbs – West Side

Aok Fitness ★★★★☆

"...34 classes per week offered... classes are challenging and fun... the staff is knowledgeable and friendly... group exercise, cycling, personal training and child care... this place has it all!...**"**

Prenatal	✗	$$$	Prices
Mommy & me	✗	❺	Decor
Child care available	✓	❸	Customer service

WWW.AOKFITNESS.COM

STRONGSVILLE—13281 PROSPECT RD (AT WESTWOOD DR); 440.268.9210; CALL FOR SCHEDULES; PARKING LOT

Berea Rec Center ★★☆☆☆

"...price is cheap if you live in Berea... unfortunately, they do not have any aerobics classes or anything... if you are into weights and equipment or swimming, then this is for you...**"**

Prenatal	✗	$	Prices
Mommy & me	✗	❷	Decor
Child care available	✓	❸	Customer service

WWW.BEREAOHIO.COM/CITYHALL/RECREATION/INDEX.CFM

BEREA—451 FRONT ST (AT FILLIER ST); 440.826.5890; CHECK SCHEDULE ONLINE; PARKING LOT

Ehrnfelt Recreation Center ★★★★☆

"...Group classes, lots of machines, and an indoor track... great pool for little ones....**"**

Prenatal	✗	$$$	Prices
Mommy & me	✗	❸	Decor
Child care available	✓	❸	Customer service

WWW.STRONGSVILLE.ORG/CONTENT/FACILITIES.ASP

STRONGSVILLE—18100 ROYALTON RD (AT ORDNER DR); 440.878.6000; CHECK SCHEDULE ONLINE; FREE PARKING

Five Seasons Country Club ★★★★☆

"...great playroom for kids... family friendly atmosphere... child care and mommy and me classes are a huge plus...**"**

Prenatal	✗	$$	Prices
Mommy & me	✓	❺	Decor
Child care available	✓	❹	Customer service

WWW.FIVESEASONSWESTLAKE.COM

WESTLAKE—28105 CLEMENS RD (AT WESTCHESTER PKWY); 440.899.4555; CHECK SCHEDULE ONLINE; PARKING LOT

Lifeworks (Southwest General Health Center) ★★★★☆

"...prenatal water and prenatal yoga for moms-to-be... LifeWorks has a terrific childcare facility for babies as young as six weeks... a beautiful pool, no waiting times for machines, indoor track, plus great instructors for many innovative classes both on land and in the water...**"**

Prenatal	✗	$	Prices
Mommy & me	✗	❺	Decor
Child care available	✓	❹	Customer service

WWW.LIFEWORKSFITNESS.NET

MIDDLEBURG HEIGHTS—7390 OLD OAK BLVD (OFF FOWLES RD); 440.816.4200; CHECK SCHEDULE ONLINE

participate in our survey at

Westlake Jazzercise Center

❝...Jazzercise combines elements of jazz dance, resistance training, Pilates, yoga, kickboxing, and more to create truly effective programs for people of every age and fitness level... always lots of fun and whips you into shape!... **❞**

Prenatal	✗	$$$	Prices
Mommy & me	✗	❸	Decor
Child care available	✗	❸	Customer service

WWW.JAZZERCISE.COM

WESTLAKE—27070 DETROIT RD (OFF RT 90); 440.871.7648; CHECK
  SCHEDULE ONLINE

YMCA

❝...the variety of fitness programs offered is astounding... class types and quality vary from facility to facility, but it's a must for new moms to check out... most facilities offer some kind of kids' activities or childcare so you can time your workouts around the classes... aerobics, yoga, pool—our Y even offers Pilates now... my favorite classes are the mom & baby yoga... the best bang for your buck... they have it all— great programs that meet the needs of a diverse range of families... **❞**

Prenatal	✓	$$	Prices
Mommy & me	✓	❸	Decor
Child care available	✓	❺	Customer service

WWW.YMCACLEVELAND.ORG

LAKEWOOD—16915 DETROIT AVE (AT CORDOVA AVE); 216.521.8400; CHECK
  SCHEDULE ONLINE

WESTLAKE—1575 COLUMBIA RD (AT HILLIARD BLVD); 440.871.6885; CHECK
  SCHEDULE ONLINE

exercise

parent education & support

Greater Cleveland Area

★★★★★

"lila picks"

★ Heights Parent Center
★ Parma Community General Hospital

Akron Children's Hospital (Baby Basics)

Childbirth classes	✗	✗ Breastfeeding support
Parent group/club	✗	✗ Child care info

WWW.AKRONCHILDRENS.ORG

AKRON—1 PERKINS SQ; 330.543.2000; CHECK SCHEDULE ONLINE

Akron City Hospital (Community Education)

Childbirth classes	✗	✓ Breastfeeding support
Parent group/club	✗	✗ Child care info

WWW.SUMMAHEALTH.ORG

AKRON—525 E MARKET ST (AT ARCH ST); 800.237.8662; CALL FOR SCHEDULE

Akron General Medical Center (Women's Services)

Childbirth classes	✗	✓ Breastfeeding support
Parent group/club	✗	✗ Child care info

WWW.AKRONGENERAL.ORG

AKRON—400 WABASH AVE (AT W CEDAR ST); 330.344.6868; CALL FOR SCHEDULE

Bradley Method, The   ★★★⯪☆

❝...12 week classes that cover all of the basics of giving birth... run by individual instructors nationwide... classes differ based on the quality and experience of the instructor... they cover everything from nutrition and physical conditioning to spousal support and medication... wonderful series that can be very educational... their web site has listings of instructors on a regional basis... ❞

Childbirth classes	✓	$$$ Prices
Parent group/club	✗	❸ Class selection
Breastfeeding support	✗	❸ Staff knowledge
Child care info	✗	❸ Customer service

WWW.BRADLEYBIRTH.COM

CLEVELAND—VARIOUS LOCATIONS; 800.422.4784; CHECK SCHEDULE & LOCATIONS ONLINE

Community Care At Home

Childbirth classes	✗	✗ Breastfeeding support

Parent group/club .... ✗   ✗ ....Child care info

BEACHWOOD—24075 COMMERCE PARK RD (OFF CHAGRIN BLVD);
216.378.8660

Cuyahoga Falls General Hospital (Childbirth Education)

Childbirth classes .... ✗   ✓ .... Breastfeeding support
Parent group/club .... ✗   ✗ ....Child care info

WWW.SUMMAHEALTH.ORG

CUYAHOGA FALLS—1900 23RD ST (AT FALLS AVE); 330.971.7698; CALL FOR
SCHEDULE

Fairview Hospital (Wellness Center)

Childbirth classes .... ✗   ✓ .... Breastfeeding support
Parent group/club .... ✗   ✗ ....Child care info

WWW.FAIRVIEWHOSPITAL.ORG

ROCKY RIVER—3035 WOOSTER RD (AT CENTER RIDGE RD); 440.356.0347;
M-F 9-2

Heights Parent Center   ★★★★★

"...we love this center... they offer informal discussion groups on a
variety of topics, drop-in play and learning sessions for parents and
kids... staff is wonderfully accommodating and helpful... huge toy
lending library and parenting book resource... plus, it's an excellent
place to meet other parents... **"**

Childbirth classes .... ✓ $$ .... Prices
Parent group/club .... ✓   ❸ .... Class selection
Breastfeeding support .... ✗   ❺ .... Staff knowledge
Child care info .... ✗   ❺ .... Customer service

WWW.HEIGHTSPARENTCENTER.ORG

CLEVELAND HEIGHTS—1700 CREST RD (AT MAYFIELD RD); 216.321.0079;
CALL FOR SCHEDULE; PARKING AT SEVERN & STAUNTON RDS

Hillcrest Hospital (Birth Education)

Childbirth classes .... ✗   ✓ .... Breastfeeding support
Parent group/club .... ✓   ✗ ....Child care info

MAYFIELD HEIGHTS—6780 MAYFIELD RD (AT GATES MILLS TOWER DR);
440.312.4647; CALL FOR SCHEDULE; FREE PARKING

Huron Hospital (Women's Health Center)

Childbirth classes .... ✗   ✓ .... Breastfeeding support
Parent group/club .... ✗   ✗ ....Child care info

WWW.HURONHOSPITAL.ORG

CLEVELAND—13951 TERRACE RD (AT BELMORE RD); 216.761.7281; CALL
FOR SCHEDULE

Lakewood Hospital (Birthing Center)

Childbirth classes .... ✗   ✓ .... Breastfeeding support
Parent group/club .... ✗   ✗ ....Child care info

WWW.LAKEWOODHOSPITAL.ORG

LAKEWOOD—1450 BELLE AVE (AT DETROIT AVE); 216.529.7762; CALL FOR
SCHEDULE

parent education & support

Lamaze International

"...thousands of women each year are educated about the birth process by Lamaze educators... their web site offers a list of local instructors... they follow a basic curriculum, but invariably class quality will depend on the individual instructor... in many ways they've set the standard for birth education classes... **"**

Childbirth classes	✓	$$$	Prices
Parent group/club	✗	❸	Class selection
Breastfeeding support	✗	❸	Staff knowledge
Child care info	✗	❸	Customer service

WWW.LAMAZE.ORG

CLEVELAND—VARIOUS LOCATIONS; 800.368.4404; CHECK SCHEDULE AND LOCATIONS ONLINE

Marymount Hospital (Family Life & Maternity)

Childbirth classes	✗	✓	Breastfeeding support
Parent group/club	✗	✗	Child care info

WWW.MARYMOUNT.ORG

GARFIELD HEIGHTS—12300 MCCRACKEN RD (AT HENRY ST); 216.581.9355

Medina General Hospital (Family Birthing Center)

Childbirth classes	✗	✓	Breastfeeding support
Parent group/club	✗	✗	Child care info

WWW.MEDINAHOSPITAL.ORG

MEDINA—1000 E WASHINGTON ST (AT FOOTE RD); 330.721.5090; CALL FOR SCHEDULE

Mocha Moms

"...a wonderfully supportive group of women—the kind of place you'll make lifelong friends for both mother and child... a comfortable forum for bouncing ideas off of other moms with same-age children... easy to get involved and not too demanding... the annual membership dues seem a small price to pay for the many activities, play groups, field trips, Moms Nights Out and book club meetings... local chapters in cities nationwide... **"**

Childbirth classes	✗	$$$	Prices
Parent group/club	✓	❸	Class selection
Breastfeeding support	✗	❸	Staff knowledge
Child care info	✗	❸	Customer service

WWW.MOCHAMOMS.ORG

CLEVELAND—VARIOUS LOCATIONS

MOMS Club

"...an international nonprofit with lots of local chapters and literally tens of thousands of members... designed to introduce you to new mothers with same-age kids wherever you live... they organize all sorts of activities and provide support for new mothers with babies... very inexpensive for all the activities you get... book clubs, moms night out, play group connections... generally a very diverse group of women... **"**

Childbirth classes	✗	$$$	Prices
Parent group/club	✓	❸	Class selection
Breastfeeding support	✗	❸	Staff knowledge
Child care info	✗	❸	Customer service

WWW.MOMSCLUB.ORG

CITY OF CLEVELAND—VARIOUS LOCATIONS

participate in our survey at

Mothers and More

"...a very neat support system for moms who are deciding to stay at home... a great way to get together with other moms in your area for organized activities... book clubs, play groups, even a 'mom's only' night out... local chapters offer more or less activities depending on the involvement of local moms..."

Childbirth classes	✗	$$$ .... Prices
Parent group/club	✓	❸ .... Class selection
Breastfeeding support	✗	❸ .... Staff knowledge
Child care info	✗	❸ .... Customer service

WWW.MOTHERSANDMORE.COM

CLEVELAND—VARIOUS LOCATIONS; CHECK SCHEDULE & LOCATIONS ONLINE

Parma Community General Hospital (Health Education Center)

"...their 'Small Wonders' Maternity Center offers an extensive array of great ... CPR, sibling classes, breastfeeding and more... the staff is experienced and very good at conducting interesting sessions... a great source of information for new parents..."

Childbirth classes	✓	$$ .... Prices
Parent group/club	✗	❹ .... Class selection
Breastfeeding support	✓	❹ .... Staff knowledge
Child care info	✗	❹ .... Customer service

WWW.PARMAHOSPITAL.ORG

CLEVELAND—7007 POWERS BLVD (AT RIDGE RD); 440.743.4030; CALL FOR SCHEDULE

PTA

"...for newborn through preshool-age children and their parents... organized through the local school system... a great way for your kids to make friends who will be in the same schools for years to come... worth joining simply because they'll match you up with a play group... they often host inexpensive kid's parties, one-time trials of dance and music classes... events during the day, evening and weekends... also great parent-only events..."

Childbirth classes	✗	$$$ .... Prices
Parent group/club	✓	❸ .... Class selection
Breastfeeding support	✗	❸ .... Staff knowledge
Child care info	✗	❸ .... Customer service

AVON LAKE— WWW.AVONLAKESCHOOLS.COM/DISTRICT/ALPTA/HOME

WWW.OHIOPTA.ORG

BEREA—VARIOUS LOCATIONS; 614.781.6344

BROOK PARK— WWW.MYSCHOOLONLINE.COM/OH/BPECPTA

BRUNSWICK— WWW.MYSCHOOLONLINE.COM/OH/BRUNSICKPRESCHOOLPTA

LAKEWOOD— WWW.LKWDPL.ORG/ECPTA/

MEDINA— WWW.CCWEBTALK.COM/MECPTA/

NORTH ROYALTON— WWW.MYSCHOOLONLINE.COM/OH/NRECPTA

OLMSTED FALLS—26944 SOUTHWOOD LANE ; 614.781.6344

ROCKY RIVER— WWW.RRECPTA.ORG

TWINSBURG— WWW.OHIOPTA.ORG; 440.914.0068

STRONGSVILLE— WWW.OHIOPTA.ORG/; 440.572.0501

WESTLAKE— WWW.MYSCHOOLONLINE.COM/OH/WECPTA

WILLOUGHBY HILLS— WWW.MYSCHOOLONLINE.COM/OH/WHECPTA

parent education & support

Rainbow Babies & Children's Hospital

Childbirth classes .... ✗   ✗ .... Breastfeeding support
Parent group/club .... ✗   ✗ .... Child care info

WWW.RAINBOWBABIES.ORG

CLEVELAND—11100 EUCLID AVE (AT CORNELL RD); 216.844.3911; CALL FOR
  SCHEDULE

Simply Done Dinners

Childbirth classes .... ✗   ✗ .... Breastfeeding support
Parent group/club .... ✗   ✗ .... Child care info

WWW.SIMPLYDONEDINNERS.COM/

PARMA—7866 BROADVIEW RD (AT W SPRAGUE RD); 216.901.0215

Southwest General Health Center

Childbirth classes .... ✗   ✓ .... Breastfeeding support
Parent group/club .... ✗   ✗ .... Child care info

WWW.SWGENERAL.COM

MIDDLEBURG HEIGHTS—18697 BAGLEY RD (AT OLD OAK BLVD);
  440.816.8035; CALL FOR SCHEDULE

UHHS Bedford Medical Center

Childbirth classes .... ✗   ✓ .... Breastfeeding support
Parent group/club .... ✓   ✗ .... Child care info

WWW.UHHSBMC.COM

CLEVELAND—44 BLAINE AVE (AT WARRENSVILLE CTR RD); 216.844.4000;
  CALL FOR SCHEDULE; FREE PARKING

UHHS Chagrin Highlands Medical Center

Childbirth classes .... ✗   ✓ .... Breastfeeding support
Parent group/club .... ✓   ✗ .... Child care info

WWW.MACDONALDWOMENSHOSPITAL.ORG

ORANGE VILLAGE—3909 ORANGE PL (AT HARVARD RD); 216.844.4000; CALL
  FOR SCHEDULE

UHHS Chesterland Health Center

Childbirth classes .... ✗   ✓ .... Breastfeeding support
Parent group/club .... ✓   ✗ .... Child care info

WWW.UHHS.COM

CHESTERLAND—8055 MAYFIELD RD (AT LASER BLVD); 216.844.4000; CALL
  FOR SCHEDULE

UHHS Geauga Regional Hospital

Childbirth classes .... ✗   ✓ .... Breastfeeding support
Parent group/club .... ✓   ✗ .... Child care info

WWW.UHHS.COM

CHARDON—13207 RAVENNA RD (AT NANTUCKET DR); 216.844.4000; CALL
  FOR SCHEDULE

UHHS Mentor Medical Center

Childbirth classes .... ✗   ✓ .... Breastfeeding support
Parent group/club .... ✓   ✗ .... Child care info

WWW.UHHS.COM

participate in our survey at

MENTOR—9000 MENTOR AVE (AT HOPKINS RD); 216.844.4000; CALL FOR
  SCHEDULE

UHHS Westlake Medical
Center

Childbirth classes .... ✗   ✓ .... Breastfeeding support
Parent group/club .... ✓   ✗ .... Child care info

WWW.UHHS.COM

WESTLAKE—960 CLAGUE RD (AT DETROIT RD); 216.844.4000; CALL FOR
  SCHEDULE

University MacDonald
Women's Hospital

Childbirth classes .... ✗   ✓ .... Breastfeeding support
Parent group/club .... ✓   ✗ .... Child care info

WWW.MACDONALDWOMENSHOSPITAL.ORG

CLEVELAND—11100 EUCLID AVE (AT ADELBERT RD); 216.844.3911; CALL
  FOR SCHEDULE

parent education & support

pediatricians

Editor's Note: Pediatricians provide a tremendous breadth of services and are very difficult to classify and rate in a brief guide. For this reason we list only those practices for which we received overwhelmingly positive reviews. We hope this list of pediatricians will help you in your search.

Greater Cleveland Area

Green Road Pediatrics

WWW.GREENROADPEDIATRICS.YOURMD.COM

CLEVELAND—1611 S GREEN RD (AT NEVILLE RD); 216.382.3800; M-F 9-5 SA
9-12; PARKING AT UNIV SUBURBAN HEALTH CTR

Hillcrest Pediatrics Inc

CLEVELAND—6770 MAYFIELD RD (AT SOM CENTER RD); 440.473.0010

Isabelita, Guadiz MD

NORTH OLMSTED—24700 LORAIN RD (AT COLUMBIA RD); 440.716.9810; M-
F 9-5; PARKING BEHIND BLDG

Kids In The Sun

WWW.KIDSINTHESUN.COM

STRONGSVILLE—18181 PEARL RD (AT DRAKE RD); 440.816.4950; M-F 9-5 SA
9-12

Lakewood Pediatrics

LAKEWOOD—14701 DETROIT AVE (AT ST CHARLES); 216.227.1330; M W F
9:30-5, T TH 9:30-1, SA 9:30-12

Murphy, Mary MD

STRONGSVILLE—16000 PEARL RD (AT KNOWLTON PKWY); 440.846.7481; M-
F 9-5

Neighborhood Pediatrics LLC

LAKEWOOD—14601 DETROIT AVE (AT BELLE AVE); 216.221.5901; M-F 8:30-
5; GARAGE @ BELLE AVE

Pediatric Services

BRUNSWICK—3812 CENTER RD (AT KENT DR); 330.225.6374; M-F 8:30-5

Pediatrics Services / UPCP

CLEVELAND—6707 POWERS BLVD (AT RIDGE RD); 440.845.1500; M-W 8-
5:30, TH-F 8-4:30, SA 8:30-12:30, SU 8:30-11; PARKING IN FRONT OF
BLDG

Senders & Associates

WWW.SENDERSRESEARCH.COM

UNIVERSITY HEIGHTS—2226 WARRENSVILLE CENTER RD (OFF CEDAR RD);
216.291.9210; M F 8:30-5, T-TH 8:30-7, SA-SU 9-12

participate in our survey at

breast pump sales & rentals

Greater Cleveland Area

★★★★★
"lila picks"

★Medic Drug

Babies R Us ★★★☆☆

"...*Medela pumps, Boppy pillows and lots of other breastfeeding supplies... staff knowledge varies from store to store, but everyone was friendly and helpful... clean and well-stocked... not a huge selection, but what they've got is great and very competitively priced...* **"**

Customer Service ....❸ $$$..Prices
WWW.BABIESRUS.COM

AURORA—7055 MARKET PL DR (AT THE 4 CORNERS PLZ); 330.995.4725; M-SA 9:30-9:30, SU 11-7; PARKING LOT

MENTOR—7841 MENTOR AVE (AT MENTOR CITY SHOPPING CTR); 440.974.7388; M-SA 9:30-9:30, SU 11-7; PARKING LOT

NORTH OLMSTED—26520 LORAIN RD (AT GREAT NORTHERN MALL); 440.716.8614; M-SA 9:30-9:30, SU 11-7; PARKING LOT

Hillcrest Hospital (Lactation Support)

WWW.HILLCRESTHOSPITAL.ORG

MAYFIELD HEIGHTS—6780 MAYFIELD RD (AT GATES MILLS TOWER DR); 440.312.5332; CALL FOR SCHEDULE; FREE PARKING

Medic Drug ★★★★★

"...*the best and most convenient way to rent a pump in the area... the pharmacy staff is polite and very knowledgeable... they really took the time to explain the ins and outs of the Medela pump I rented... several models available to rent or buy... their service was good and the prices were reasonable ($55-$65 per month depending on the model)...* **"**

Customer Service ....❸ $$$..Prices
WWW.MEDICDRUG.COM

BAY VILLAGE—27251 WOLF RD (AT DOVER CTR); 440.835.1450; M-SA 8-9, SU 9-5; FREE PARKING

BEDFORD—647 BROADWAY AVE (AT COLUMBUS RD); 440.232.6500; M-SA 8-9, SU 9-5; FREE PARKING

BRECKSVILLE—8966 BRECKSVILLE RD (AT ARLINGTON ST); 440.526.5250; M-F 8-10, SU 9-7

CHAGRIN FALLS—9535 TANGLEWOOD SQ (AT BAINBRIDGE RD); 440.543.9895; M-SA 9-9, SU 9-5

CLEVELAND—17400 LORAIN AVE (AT ROCKY RIVER RD); 216.671.3100; M-SA 8-9, SU 9-5

CLEVELAND—4507 CLARK AVE (AT W 44TH); 216.651.2022; M-F 8-9, SA 9-9, SU 9-5

CLEVELAND—709 E 185TH ST (AT HILLER AVE); 216.481.4165; M-SA 9-9, SU 9-5

CLEVELAND HEIGHTS—1833 COVENTRY RD (AT MAYFIELD RD); 216.321.1611; M-SA 9-12, SU 9-5

EUCLID—19001 EUCLID AVE (AT E 191ST ST); 216.531.1466; M-F 9-9, SU 9-5

GARFIELD HEIGHTS—12000 MCCRACKEN RD (AT E 126TH ST); 216.662.6466; M-F 8-6, SA 9-2

GARFIELD HEIGHTS—4790 TURNEY RD (AT GARFIELD BLVD); 216.883.1009; M-SA 9-9, SU 9-5

LAKEWOOD—18200 SLOANE AVE (AT W CLIFTON BLVD); 216.228.2500; M-SA 9-10, SU 9-5

MAPLE HEIGHTS—15780 BROADWAY (AT LIBBY RD); 216.587.6780; M-SA 9-9, SU 9-5

MENTOR—7320 LAKESHORE BLVD (AT RTE 206); 440.946.7978; M-SA 8-10, SU 9-9

MIDDLEBURG HEIGHTS—15250 E BAGLEY RD (AT RT 206); 440.886.0700; M-SA 9-9, SU 9-5

PARMA—10407 PLEASANT VALLEY RD (AT PEARL RD); 440.842.5422; M-SA 9-9, SU 9-5

PARMA—5510 RIDGE RD (AT PEARL RD); 440.845.8555; M-SA 8-10, SU 9-5

SHAKER HEIGHTS—20145 VAN AKEN BLVD (AT WARRENSVILLE CTR); 216.921.8700; M-SA 7-12, SU 9-5

SOLON—34362 AURORA RD (E OF SOM CTR RD); 440.248.6500; M-SA 8-10, SU 9-6

STRONGSVILLE—17100 ROYALTON RD (AT SOM CTR RD); 440.238.5505; M-SA 9-9, SU 9-5

WICKLIFFE—29420 EUCLID AVE (AT ROCKEFELLER); 440.943.0656; M-SA 9-9, SU 9-5

WILLOWICK—30450 LAKESHORE BLVD (AT E 305TH); 440.944.0691; M-SA 9-9, SU 9-5

USA Baby

WWW.USABABY.COM

CUYAHOGA FALLS—2929 STATE RD (AT GRAHAM RD); 330.928.2229; M-T TH 10-8, W F-SA 10-6, SU 12-4; FREE PARKING

WESTLAKE—25027 CENTER RIDGE RD (AT KING JAMES PKWY); 440.835.9696; M-T TH 10-8, W F-SA 10-6, SU 12-5; PARKING LOT

diaper delivery

Online

amazon.com

"...I'm always amazed by the amount of stuff Amazon sells—including a pretty good selection of pumps... Medela, Avent, Isis, Ameda... prices range from great to average... pretty easy shopping experience... free shipping on bigger orders... **"**

babycenter.com

"...they carry all the major brands... prices are competitive, but keep in mind you'll need to pay for shipping too... the comments from parents are incredibly helpful... excellent customer service... easy shopping experience... **"**

birthexperience.com

"...Medela and Avent products... great deal with the Canadian currency conversion... get free shipping with big orders... easy site to navigate... **"**

breast-pumps.com

breastmilk.com

ebay.com

"...you can get Medela pumps brand new in packaging with the warranty for $100 less than retail... able to buy immediately instead of having to bid and wait... wide variety... be sure to check for shipping price... great place to find deals, but research the seller before you bid... **"**

express-yourself.net

healthchecksystems.com

lactationconnection.com

"...Ameda and Whisper Wear products... nice selection and competitive prices... quick delivery of any nursing or lactation product you can imagine... the selection of mom and baby related items is fantastic... **"**

medela.com

"...well worth the money... fast, courteous and responsive... great site for a full listing of Medela products and links to purchase online... quality of customer service by phone varies... licensed lactation specialist answers e-mail via email at no charge and with quick turnaround... **"**

mybreastpump.com

"...a great online one-stop-shop for all things breast feeding... you can purchase hospital grade pumps from them... fast service for all you breastfeeding needs... **"**

participate in our survey at

haircuts

Greater Cleveland Area

★★★★★
"lila picks"

- ★ Cookie Cutters Haircuts
- ★ Snip-its Haircuts For Kids

Cookie Cutters Haircuts ★★★★★

" *...great place for baby's first haircut-even a special first haircut package... a fun salon with an indoor playground in which the kids can play before and after their cuts... very clever concept and well done—it's basically the only way I can get my son's hair cut... the stylists aren't always that consistent, but they do a good enough job... nice and patient staff... this place is perfectly designed for kids who hate having their haircut... my kids refuse to go anywhere else...* **"**

Customer Service ....❹ $$...Prices

WWW.HAIRCUTSAREFUN.COM

WESTLAKE—30024 DETROIT RD (AT CROCKER RD); 440.617.1717

Gimme A Haircut ★★★★☆

" *...friendly staff and a haircut for under $10... nice cuts—nothing fancy, but the price is definitely right... we've been coming here since day one and wouldn't have it any other way...* **"**

Customer Service ....❹ $ ....Prices

MEDINA—860 N COURT ST (AT HARDING ST); 330.725.4222; M-F 9-9, SA 9-6, SU 10-4

Kids Kuts ★★★☆☆

" *...great place for first haircut... videos and other distractions for the kids... fun place for the kids, but haircuts are only fair... a little dusty and old... I've heard some bad experiences, and some good ones...* **"**

Customer Service ....❹ $$$.......................................Prices

ROCKY RIVER—19524 CENTER RIDGE RD (AT WOOSTER RD); 440.333.2887

Ladies & Gentlemen Salon

LYNDHURST—25377 CEDAR RD (AT RICHMOND RD); 216.291.0489

MENTOR—8800 MENTOR AVE (AT JACKSON ST); 440.255.5572

Sausalito Salon ★★★★☆

" *...they have a motorcycle for the kids to ride and videos for them to watch while they're getting their haircut... of course there's also the requisite lollipop at the end as well...* **"**

Customer Service ....❹ $$...Prices

BEACHWOOD—2101 RICHMOND RD (AT CEDAR RD); 216.591.9010

Snip-its Haircuts For Kids

"...the entertainment is unbeatable... kids' haircuts without all the stress... the only place we ever go... quick, painless and relatively cheap... they really know kids and how to keep them entertained while snipping away... they do a fabulous job... long waits (can be an hour or more) and they don't take appointments unless you join a VIP club... bubbles, videos, games and lollipops kept my daughter busy throughout the cut... patient stylists who know all the tricks to put your little one at ease... pricey, but worth it for a stylist used to squirming kids..."

Customer Service................. ❸ $$$ .... Prices
WWW.SNIPITS.COM
HUDSON—89 1ST ST (AT OWEN BROWN ST); 330.653.3353; M-SA 10-7 SU 12-5

haircuts

nanny & babysitter referrals

Greater Cleveland Area

Childcare Solutions ★★★☆☆

"...they do a great job... wonderful nannies, and nice that they interview to match them to your needs... **"**

Baby nurses	✗	$$	Prices
Nannies	✓	❹	Candidate selection
Au pairs	✗	❹	Staff knowledge
Babysitters	✗	❹	Customer service

WWW.4INHOMECARE.COM

BEACHWOOD— (AT 2101 RICHMOND RD); 216.831.7333

English Nanny & Governess School

Baby nurses	✗	✓	Nannies
Au pairs	✗	✗	Babysitters

WWW.NANNY-GOVERNESS.COM

CHAGRIN FALLS—37 S FRANKLIN ST (AT CTR ST); 800.733.1984

Erin's Nannies

Baby nurses	✗	✓	Nannies
Au pairs	✗	✗	Babysitters

BEACHWOOD—24300 CHAGRIN BLVD (AT RICHMOND RD); 216.514.3600

John Carroll University ★★★☆☆

"...a free service helps you recruit a babysitter from the college... a little low tech—you put your name and requirements in a book and interested students can phone you—but overall an effective way to find a competent sitter without an expensive service!... **"**

Baby nurses	✗	$	Prices
Nannies	✗	❹	Candidate selection
Au pairs	✗	❹	Staff knowledge
Babysitters	✓	❹	Customer service

Service Area ...Greater Cleveland area

WWW.JCU.EDU

UNIVERSITY HEIGHTS—20700 N PARK BLVD (AT FAIRMOUNT BLVD); 216.397.1886

Sondra's Nanny Care

Baby nurses	✓	✓	Nannies
Au pairs	✗	✓	Babysitters

Service Area ...Greater Cleveland area

PAINESVILLE—6964 PENNYWHISTLE CIR (AT BRIGHTWOOD DR); 440.796.8463

Starting Point For Child Care ★★★★☆

"...starting point provides a great list of questions that can be used by parents when interviewing potential child care providers... the free referral service is a great place to start your search... **"**

Baby nurses	✓	$	Prices
Nannies	✓	❹	Candidate selection
Au pairs	✗	❹	Staff knowledge
Babysitters	✗	❹	Customer service

WWW.STARTING-POINT.ORG

CLEVELAND—2000 E 9TH ST (AT EUCLID AVE); 216.575.0061

participate in our survey at

The Nanny Place

Baby nurses.................................. ✗   ✓ ....Nannies
Au pairs....................................... ✗   ✗ ....Babysitters
Service Area...............West Side only

WESTLAKE—29799 HILLIARD OAK LN (AT HILLIARD BLVD); 440.892.7868

nanny & babysitter referrals

Online

★ ★ ★ ★ ★

"lila picks"

★ craigslist.org

4nannies.com

Baby nurses	✗	✓	Nannies
Au pairs	✗	✗	Babysitters

Service Area ....nationwide
WWW.4NANNIES.COM

aupaircare.com

Baby nurses	✗	✗	Nannies
Au pairs	✓	✗	Babysitters

Service Area ....International
WWW.AUPAIRCARE.COM

aupairinamerica.com

Baby nurses	✗	✗	Nannies
Au pairs	✓	✗	Babysitters

Service Area ....International
WWW.AUPAIRINAMERICA.COM

babysitters.com

Baby nurses	✗	✗	Nannies
Au pairs	✗	✓	Babysitters

Service Area ....nationwide
WWW.BABYSITTERS.COM

craigslist.org ★ ★ ★ ★ ★

❝...you can find just about anything on craigslist... good starting point, especially if you don't want to spend a lot of money and are willing to do your own screening... we received at least 50 responses to our 'nanny wanted' ad... helped me find very qualified baby-sitters... includes all major cities in the US... ❞

Baby nurses	✓	✓	Nannies
Au pairs	✗	✓	Babysitters

WWW.CRAIGSLIST.ORG

enannysource.com

Baby nurses	✗	✓	Nannies
Au pairs	✗	✗	Babysitters

Service Area ....nationwide
WWW.ENANNYSOURCE.COM

findcarenow.com

Baby nurses	✗	✗	Nannies
Au pairs	✗	✓	Babysitters

Service Area ....nationwide
WWW.FINDCARENOW.COM

get-a-sitter.com

Baby nurses .... ✗   ✗ .... Nannies
Au pairs .... ✗   ✓ .... Babysitters
Service Area .... nationwide
WWW.GET-A-SITTER.COM

householdstaffing.com

Baby nurses .... ✓   ✓ .... Nannies
Au pairs .... ✗   ✗ .... Babysitters
WWW.HOUSEHOLDSTAFFING.COM

interexchange.org

Baby nurses .... ✗   ✗ .... Nannies
Au pairs .... ✓   ✗ .... Babysitters
Service Area .... International
WWW.INTEREXCHANGE.ORG

nannies4hire.com

Baby nurses .... ✗   ✓ .... Nannies
Au pairs .... ✗   ✗ .... Babysitters
WWW.NANNIES4HIRE.COM

nannylocators.com   ★★★⯪☆

❝...many listings of local nannies available... I have found that the
listings are not always up to date... $100 subscriber fee to respond and
contact nannies that have posted... different regions have varying
amounts of listings available... **❞**

Baby nurses .... ✗   ✓ .... Nannies
Au pairs .... ✗   ✗ .... Babysitters
Service Area .... Nationwide
WWW.NANNYLOCATORS.COM

sittercity.com   ★★★★☆

❝...Wonderful online resource... an online baby-sitter database filled
with mostly college and graduate students looking for baby-sitting and
nanny jobs... candidates are not prescreened so you must check
references... Fee to access the database is $35 plus $5 per month...
tends to be be more useful for baby-sitters than regular daytime
nannies... **❞**

Baby nurses .... ✗   ✗ .... Nannies
Au pairs .... ✗   ✓ .... Babysitters
Service Area .... nationwide
WWW.SITTERCITY.COM

student-sitters.com

Baby nurses .... ✗   ✗ .... Nannies
Au pairs .... ✗   ✓ .... Babysitters
WWW.STUDENT-SITTERS.COM

nanny & babysitter referrals

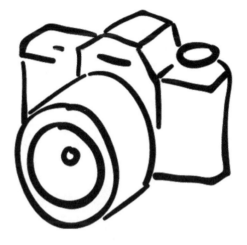

photographers

Greater Cleveland Area

★★★★★

"lila picks"

★Kiddie Kandids

Humbert Studio

WWW.PHOTOREFLECT.COM/SCRIPTS/PRSM.DLL?STOREFRONT?B=1&C=05R2
CLEVELAND—16205 LORAIN AVE (AT W 162ND ST); 216.251.5600

JB Focus

MEDINA—616 WADSWORTH RD (AT SPRINGBROOK DR); 330.722.3773

JCPenney Portrait Studio ★★★⯪☆

❝...don't expect works of art, but they are great for a quick wallet photo... photographers and staff range from great to not so good... a quick portrait with standard props and backdrops... definitely join the portrait club and use coupons... waits are especially long around the holidays, so consider taking your Christmas pictures early... the e-picture option is a time saver... wait time for prints can be up to a month... look for coupons and you'll never have to pay full price...❞

Customer service......................❹ $$..Prices

WWW.JCPPORTRAITS.COM

AKRON—600 CHAPEL HILL MALL (AT INDEPENDENCE AVE); 330.633.5698

ELYRIA—380 MIDWAY MALL (AT LORAIN BLVD); 440.324.6677

MENTOR—7850 MENTOR AVE (AT GREAT LAKE MALL); 440.974.6411

NORTH OLMSTED—5100 GREAT NORTHERN MALL (AT GREAT NORTHERN BLVD); 440.777.4767

PARMA—7900 DAY DR (AT PARMATOWN SHOPPING CTR); 440.845.9127

STRONGSVILLE—SOUTHPARK MALL (AT ON WOODLEAF RD); 440.846.8676

Kiddie Kandids ★★★★★

❝...good quality photos for all occasions... they made a big effort to get a smile out of my grumpy son... you don't need to make a reservation, just pop in and have the pictures taken... no sitting fee... photographers take the extra time necessary to get a great shot and they have the cutest props... lots of items to buy with your pictures on them—cups, bags, mouse pads... buy the CD of pictures rather than buying the prints... pictures are available right after the sitting...❞

Customer service......................❹ $$$..Prices

WWW.KIDDIEKANDIDS.COM

NORTH OLMSTED—26520 LORAIN RD (AT BROOKPARK RD); 440.716.9830

Moto Photo ★★★★⯪

❝...good photos at a reasonable price... quick service and a photot club where sittings are free... ask for Greg...❞

Customer service......................❹ $$$..Prices

WWW.MOTOPHOTO.COM

CLEVELAND HEIGHTS—13998 CEDAR RD (AT WARRENSVILLE CTR RD);
216.321.2525

SHAKER HEIGHTS—20141 VAN AKEN BLVD (AT WARRENSVILLE CTR RD);
216.751.6686

Nelson's Photography Studios

"...the photographer has children of her own and works very well with kids... tries a variety of poses to get a good picture... professional and friendly staff—the whole process was fun and enjoyable..."

Customer service .... **❺** $$$ .... Prices

WWW.NELSONSPHOTOUSA.COM

MIDDLEBURG HEIGHTS—6886 PEARL RD (AT SOUTHLAND SHOPPING CTR);
440.845.6900; CALL FOR APPT

ROCKY RIVER—2565 WOOSTER RD (AT HILLARD BLVD); 440.333.3830; CALL
FOR APPT

Picture People

"...this well-known photography chain offers good package deals that get even better with coupons... generally friendly staff despite the often 'uncooperative' little customers... they don't produce super fancy, artistic shots, but you get your pictures in under an hour... reasonable quality for a fast portrait... kind of hit-or-miss quality and customer service..."

Customer service .... **❹** $$$ .... Prices

WWW.PICTUREPEOPLE.COM

AKRON—2000 BRITTAIN RD (AT CHAPEL HILLS); 330.634.0410; M-SA 10-9,
SU 12-6

AKRON—3265 W MARKET ST (AT SUMMIT MALL); 330.865.7610; M-SA 10-9,
SU 11-6

BEACHWOOD—26300 CEDAR RD (AT BEACHWOOD PLACE MALL);
216.292.2347

ELYRIA—4539 MIDWAY MALL (AT LORAIN BLVD); 440.324.2347; M-SA 10-9,
SU 11-6

MENTOR—7850 MENTOR AVE (AT GREAT LAKES); 440.974.9800; M-SA 10-9,
SU 11-6

NORTH OLMSTED—GREAT NORTHERN MALL (AT BROOKPARK RD);
440.716.8812

PARMA—7897 W RIDGWOOD DR (AT PARMATOWN); 440.845.6633

Sears Portrait Studio

"...the price is right, but the service and quality are variable... make an appointment to cut down on the wait time... bring your coupons for even better prices... perfect for getting a nice wallet size portrait without spending a fortune... I wish the wait time for prints wasn't so long (2 weeks)... the quality and service-orientation of the photographers really vary a lot—some are great, some aren't..."

Customer service .... **❸** $$ .... Prices

WWW.SEARSPORTRAIT.COM

AKRON—2000 BRITTAIN RD (AT HOWE AVE IN CHAPEL HILL MALL);
330.633.8085; M-SA 10-8, SU 11-5

MENTOR—7875 JOHNNYCAKE RIDGE RD (AT DEEPWOOD BLVD IN GREAT
LAKE MALL); 440.255.3442

MIDDLEBURG HEIGHTS—6950 W 130TH ST (AT SOUTHLAND SHOPPING
CTR); 440.845.5488; M-F 10-8, SA 9-8, SU 11-5

NORTH OLMSTED—5000 GREAT NORTHERN BLVD (AT BROOKPARK RD);
440.779.5422

NORTH RANDALL—501 RANDALL PARK MALL (AT EMERY RD); 216.663.7487;
   M-F 10-8, SA 9-8, SU 11-5

STRONGSVILLE—17271 SOUTHPARK CTR (AT ROYALTON RD); 440.846.0983

Online

clubphoto.com
WWW.CLUBPHOTO.COM

dotphoto.com
WWW.DOTPHOTO.COM

flickr.com
WWW.FLICKR.COM

kodakgallery.com

"...the popular ofoto.com is now under it's wings... very easy to use desktop software to upload your pictures on their site... prints, books, mugs and other photo gifts are reasonably priced and are always shipped promptly... I like that there is no limit to how many pictures and albums you can have their site... **"**

WWW.KODAKGALLERY.COM

photoworks.com
WWW.PHOTOWORKS.COM

shutterfly.com

"...I've spent hundreds of dollars with them—it's so easy and the quality of the pictures is great... they use really nice quality photo paper... what a lifesaver—since I store all of my pictures with them I didn't lose any when my computer crashed... most special occasions are take care of with a personal photo calendar, book or other item with the cutest pictures of our kids... reasonable prices... **"**

WWW.SHUTTERFLY.COM

snapfish.com

"...great photo quality and never a problem with storage limits... we love their photo books and flip books—easy to make and fun to give... good service and a good price... we have family that lives all over the country and yet everyone still gets to see and order pictures of our new baby... **"**

WWW.SNAPFISH.COM

indexes

alphabetical

by city/neighborhood

alphabetical

participate in our survey at

by city/neighborhood

participate in our survey at

Notes

Notes

otes

Notes

Notes

Notes

Notes

es

Notes

Notes